The **COMPACT TRACTOR BIBLE**

The COMPACT TRACTOR BIBLE

DR. GRAEME R. QUICK

Voyageur
Press

First published in 2006 by Voyageur Press, an imprint of MBI Publishing Company, Galtier Plaza, Suite 200, 380 Jackson Street, St. Paul, MN 55101-3885 USA

MBI Publishing Company titles are also available at discounts in bulk quantity for industrial or sales-promotional use. For details write to Special Sales Manager at MBI Publishing Company, Galtier Plaza, Suite 200, 380 Jackson Street, St. Paul, MN 55101-3885 USA

Editor: Amy Glaser
Designer: Christopher Fayers

Printed in China

Library of Congress Cataloging-in-Publication Data

Quick, Graeme R.
  The compact tractor bible / Graeme R. Quick.
    p. cm. -- (Country workshop series)
  Includes index.
  ISBN-13: 978-0-7603-2393-9 (pbk. : alk. paper)
  ISBN-10: 0-7603-2393-3 (pbk. : alk. paper)
  1. Garden tractors. 2. Lawn tractors. I. Title. II. Series.
  S711.Q85 2006
  629.225'2--dc22
                                                        2006015734

About the Author:
Dr. Graeme Quick recently completed a seven-year term as Leader, Power & Machinery Engineering Section and Adjunct Professor, Agricultural & Biosystems Engineering Department, Iowa State University. He is currently a consulting engineer based in Queensland, Australia.

On the front cover:
Main image: Deere's versatile Model 2305 provides great utility and enhances the pleasure of living on a hobby farm or acreage.

Detail image: Routine maintenance is an important aspect of keeping your compact tractor in good running order.

On the back cover:
Kubota Models B2630 and B3030 showing TLB and ROPS, bare FWA tractor with ROPS and grille guard, and full cab and mid-mount mower options.

CONTENTS

INTRODUCTION

SELECTING AND USING COMPACT TRACTORS AND THEIR WORKING ATTACHMENTS

Five Ps: price, power, parts, performance, and prestige are key factors in selecting a compact tractor or riding mower. This book objectively examines each factor in simple language. If you're in the market for a compact piece of mobile equipment, you will quickly discover that there are many choices. There are at least 88 brands of compact tractors, riding mowers, and compact mobile equipment offered nationally, and there are many models within those brands.

Renting, leasing, and hiring contractors are alternatives to buying. This book will save you trouble and money with details on:

• Quantifying job requirements
• Deciding what attachments are needed
• Matching compact equipment to the job
• Measuring performance objectively
• Calculating costs to own and operate
• Settling whether to buy, lease, rent a machine, or contract out the job
• Buying secondhand
• Pleasure and safety aspects
• What future compact machines might look like

A useful reference section is appended, along with an index. This book is an invaluable guide for residential and acreage owners, contractors, and professionals—anyone selecting and working with compact tractors, smaller mobile equipment and tool carriers, and their attachments.

CHAPTER 1
WHAT IS A COMPACT TRACTOR?

Definition: A compact tractor is a mobile machine that meets a need for a versatile, self-driving compact power unit and tool carrier for working smaller areas.

The word "tractor" has Latin roots and is derived from *trahere* meaning to pull, draw, or drag. Many tractor jobs involve pulling equipment from the drawbar, but that's only a starting point. As for the meaning of "compact," there is no rigid definition, but the industry seems to have set the bar generally at tractors up to 55 engine horsepower (41 kw).

Over the years the engine power of tractors has steadily increased. There was a time within living memory when a Fordson, Farmall, or Ferguson/Ford was the main farm tractor, and they were rated 19 to 28 horsepower at the flywheel! The average power of compacts is climbing relentlessly. This book will use the above definition, and allowing for power creep over time, will stay below 75 horsepower for compact tractors, mowing tractors, and mobile machines that use tractor technologies.

The book will not deal with recreational all-terrain vehicles (ATVs) or higher-powered machines used for broadacre farming or other large-scale agricultural operations. The focus is on compact tractors and the mobile power equipment used on areas by hobby and small-scale farmers, contractors, and in the rental trade.

The word "compact" is useful, but it does not appear on any recognized machinery standards. Other tractor prefixes like mini, subcompact, utility, estate, compact utility, and some other colorful labels are bandied around, but they have no standard tractor power ranges. None of those words will be used as definitions in this book, whereas the word "compact" will distinguish such tractors from larger machines. Commercial versus residential or consumer products are also useful ways to distinguish their use.

SPECIAL POWER TAKE-OFF (PTO) FOR LAWN AND GARDEN TRACTORS

The American Society of Agricultural Engineers (ASAE) in the relevant PTO standards defines a lawn and garden ride-on tractor as a "self-propelled machine, designed and advertised for general-purpose lawn and garden work." The standards list the distinguishing characteristics of this type of

machine; the 2,000-rpm PTO was intended for transmitting power up to 27 horsepower (20 kw). Refer to ASAE Standards S323 and S370, respectively. These standards at least put a power rating on one class of smaller tractors—for now!

LIST OF COMPACT TRACTOR MAKERS OR BRANDS AVAILABLE

The past decade has been a remarkable one for compact tractors in the United States, with a 308 percent increase in sales between 1995 and 2004, of tractors under 40 horsepower. By comparison, wheeled agricultural tractor sales in the 40 to 100 horsepower bracket increased 80 percent over the same period. In 2004, the under-50 horsepower wheeled-tractor market was worth more than $2 billion, and that does not include parts and service value, or riding mowers. The total market for compact tractors, riding mowers, smaller skid steers, etc., is estimated to be around 350,000 sold per year in the United States, and that number is holding well. Riding mowers alone, with over 100,000 machines sold, are worth $3 billion annually. There may be around 20 million compact tractors in use in the United States. The sales, parts, and service business for such numbers is significant, with several dealers in practically every town.

There are 88 makes or brands of compact tractors, mini-loaders, and ride-on machines available in North America. Most of these brands offer information on their respective websites. There are more than 40 brands of mowers, and 33 types of zero-turn mowers alone were listed in *Landscape Management* magazine in 2004. Many compact machine brands have a dozen or more models. The number of model options available exceeds a thousand! This book will help you find the best choice for your application.

COMPACT TRACTOR SYSTEMATICS

A wit once said, "I can work as much land as my wife can weed!" That was in a place where everything had to be done manually. Without powered equipment, a person can only work an acre of land, or if really pushed, a couple might work two acres year round. Now we have engines and tractors and can do so much more, but sorting through today's choices calls for a systematic approach in arriving at the best solution for a given task.

Tractors are categorized in several basic ways. The broadest divisions are between residential tractors or consumer products versus commercial or professional compact tractors.

Consumer and residential products are intentionally built lighter and cheaper in anticipation that they will be worked for less hours than in a business or commercial operation. They aren't built to carry attachments, such as loaders, and when used by homeowners, they may log only 200 hours a year.

Commercial products are compact machines intended to generate an income. They are used by contractors and individuals in the light industrial/construction/building trades; by horticulturalists, landscapers, greenskeepers, golf course managers, and turf growers; and for councils and other government agencies. These commercial or professional machines are more ruggedly built and have different specifications for larger annual hours of use, such as several thousand hours a year.

The tractor weight-to-power ratios between these two groups are significantly different. For example, 88 pounds per PTO horsepower for commercial tractors compared to 35 pounds per net horsepower for consumer-type machines.

Compact tractors used around farms and in part-time, hobby farming, multiuse, and small-scale farms fall somewhere in between. They will log more hours per year than consumer or residential tractors.

Garden tractors, ride-on mowers, and tractors equipped with mowers may be the most obvious use for compact tractors, but the range certainly doesn't end there. A fast-growing area for landscaping, construction, and rental business is in dedicated tractor-loader-backhoes (TLBs), skid steers and mini-earthmovers, concrete dumpsters, work utility vehicles, and a host of attachments for those tool carriers. Labor is probably one of the greatest problems that the construction, grounds care, and greens industry faces—reliable labor is scarce and can be the highest cost item in a business. Mini-loaders can do the work of at least half a dozen laborers. They are the landscape contractor's "Swiss Army Knife." Compact equipment comes into its own to get jobs done fast with less labor. Mowing is just one of the more common jobs for compact tractors.

There are specialized tractors and equipment for orchard, vineyard, rice field, greenhouse, vegetable, and horticultural nurseries, that include low-profile, row crop, narrow, and straddle types of tractors. Slope-type tractors and tractor-mowers with fixed or tilting axles

This is a list of 88 brands of compact tractors and makers of mobile equipment that use compact tractor technologies available in North America.

Aebi	Gehl	New Holland
Ariens	Goldoni	Polaris
AGCO	Graden	Power Trac
ASV	Gravely	Ramrod
Avant	Great Dane	Ransomes
Bad Boy	Grasshopper	Rich
BCS	Hinowa	Same
Bobcat	Hinomoto	Saukville
Bolens	Honda	Scag
Boxer	Hustler	Simplicity
Bucyrus	Husqvarna	Shibaura
Bush Hog	Iseki	Snapper
Caterpillar	Jacobsen	Solo
Carraro	JCB	Steiner
Case	Jinma	Stiga
Coyote	John Deere	Swisher
Craftsman	Jonsered	Thomas
Cub Cadet	Jungle Jim	Toro
Cushman	Kanga	Tructor
DeWeze	Kioti	TSM
Dingo	Kubota	Viking
Dixie Chopper	Lamborghini	Yanmar
Dixon	Lastec	Yard-Man
East Wind	Long	Yazoo/Kees
Exmark	Mahindra	Walker
Farmall	Massey Ferguson	WMI
Ferrari	Mitsubishi	Wolf
Ferris	MTD	Woods
Finn	Murray	Wright
	Mustang	

are also available, as well as special transportation or nontraction compact tractors and utility vehicles.

Tractors are also categorized by frame type. The different types of frames include rigid, articulated, wheeled versus tracked undercarriage, and single- or multiaxle. Within the latter category, there are many options: single axle, two wheel; two-wheel drive (2WD), four-wheel drive (4WD) equal-sized wheels; 4WD with unequal-sized wheels, which is also called front-wheel assist (FWA); and multiaxle types with six and eight wheels.

Kubota

There are several track types available for tractors: Rubber tracks are either friction or sprocket driven, and add-on tracks can be placed over pneumatic tires. Steel tracks are also an option and come in high or low sprocket drives.

Tool carriers are also an important role for compact tractors.

Another categorization for tractors is by steering technology. Ackermann steering linkage is available for the front or rear axle. The linkage design prevents tire scrubbing on cornering and the axles turn on a common or virtual pivot point. Complex steering, which is featured with New Holland's SuperSteer, has Ackermann linkage as well as front-axle swivel like a wagon axle, tightening the turning circle by 40 percent. Kubota's Bi-Steer powers the front drive wheels at twice the peripheral speed of the rear wheels whenever the front wheels exceed a 35-degree turning angle. This provides a tighter, smoother turn.

Skid-steer wheels are not designed to pivot. Turning is accomplished by either braking or reversing the inside track or wheels and speeding up the outside wheels. This causes tire wear by scuffing, and there is considerable ground disturbance on soft surfaces.

ARTICULATED STEERING

Four-wheel steer (4WS) and crab steer have exceptional maneuverability around obstacles. One garden tractor manufacturer advertises a 6.5-inch inside turning radius on its 4WS machine. Crab steering is rare on compact tractors.

With caster and lever steering, one or two caster wheels rotate freely on a vertical axis. Steering is accomplished by drive-wheel speed control only and there are no steering linkages. Zero-turn machines fit in this category.

Power steering makes steering easier by using hydraulic power to boost steering signals. This feature is

Dixon

John Deere

useful on any tractor but is essential for heavy-duty vehicles, tractor loader work, and articulated vehicles.

The last category that tractors are organized by is the method of mounting attachments. These categorizations include implements or attachments towed or pulled by the drawbar; semi-, frame-, or submounted equipment; fully mounted; or mid- or belly-mounted.

WHAT CAN A COMPACT TRACTOR DO?

The compact tractor is a versatile, self-moving power unit and tool carrier. But it's what is put onto the tractor that turns it into a working machine! The tractor standing alone is not much use, unless to show off in the neighborhood as a status symbol, and that's the unquantifiable prestige factor!

Attachment options are available nowadays for compact tractors that can be adapted to do practically anything. Some makes of compact tractors have as many as 70 attachment options. Among those compacts with a very wide range of attachments are Bobcat's Toolcat, the Toro Dingo, and the Avant. Some of the more common tractor options and attachments are mowers, front-end loaders, backhoes,

Deere's versatile 2210 with number 210 loader and belly mower provides great utility and enhances the pleasure of living on a hobby farm or acreage. John Deere

John Deere fixed-frame 5420 front-wheel assist. John Deere

John Deere

11

Skid-steer loader on pneumatics. CNH

Ackermann steering on the Case FWA tractor allows the wheels to follow different radius circles on turns. CNH

rotary hoes, cultivators, plows, blades, rakes, sweepers, snow blowers, and tree spades. Most of these attachments are also used on skid steers.

ARE THERE ALTERNATIVES TO TYPICAL TRACTOR CONFIGURATIONS?

Four-wheeled tractors with two axles will occupy the bigger part of this book. Four-wheeled tractors come in single rear-axle drive, front-wheel assist (FWA), or

FWD with equal-sized wheels. Tracked tractors will be kept in this bracket for convenience. Four wheels is the usual configuration, but there are others.

Single-Axle Tractors

Operator-controlled, single-axle, or two-wheeled tractors are an option for very small areas, steep sloping land, and gardening jobs. These self-propelled machines are commonly equipped with a rotary tiller or mower, but are

Bobcat skid-steer loader with concrete breaker attachment. John Deere

adaptable to use a front rotary broom, sickle bar, light-duty chipper/shredder, pressure washer, snowplow, leaf blower, or to be hitched up with a trailer. If you travel in Southeast Asia you will see thousands of these on the roads. They are low-cost unsophisticated models, often powered by hopper-cooled, single-cylinder diesels and hitched to a trailer used to transport goods and people. Several single-axle tractor systems, including Gravely,

Aebi, and BCS, are available in the United States, with many attachment options.

Skid-Steer Loaders

Skid-steer loaders have replaced tractors for many commercial, agricultural, and landscaping applications. Originally designed to maneuver inside a barn, nowadays these agile machines can be fitted with a variety of attachments, such as a backhoe, trencher, brush cutter, posthole digger, manure forks, tiller, hay spear, or tracks for improved traction. Narrow widths and a tight turning radius make skid steers great for working in confined areas, but they are not good for lawns, unless they have rubber tracks. The mini-skid loader class is narrow enough to go through a 32-inch garden gate or door. Mini-skid loaders are essentially a mobile hydraulic platform and are well matched to the needs of landscaping contractors. They are usually operated from a rear stand-up platform so they are fast to get on or off. Attachments can be quickly changed between jobs. A complete contractor's setup fits neatly on a trailer.

Mini-excavators

Mini-excavators, used in combination with a skid steer,

JCB's Loadall 50 horsepower Model 520 has all-wheel steer. JCB Sales Limited

Aebi's Combicut CC66 has individual hydrostatic drives to each wheel for a heavy-duty, pedestrian-controlled single-axle tractor. The 18-horsepower machine is shown here with front-drive flail mower attached. AEBI

Toro Dingo can fit through the personnel door of a shed. Toro

Bobcat's Toolcat in 4WD and 4WS. Bobcat

have emerged as an economical alternative to a tractor-loader-backhoe (TLB) combination. Mini-excavators come in either tail-swing or zero tail-swing configurations. Side-shift models are available for working near or against buildings. They have astonishing capabilities in the hands of a skilled operator.

All-Terrain Vehicles (ATVs)

ATVs have a somewhat different clientele. They are capable of high speeds and are mostly for recreational use. They will not be covered in this book.

Rough Terrain Utility Vehicles (UVs)

UVs are distinguished from ATVs by virtue of being designed primarily for off-roadwork, carrying payloads, and powering equipment at lower speeds.

John Deere's Gator. John Deere

John Deere's utility vehicle. John Deere

Kubota UTV.

CHAPTER 2
SELECTING A COMPACT TRACTOR

CONSUMER VERSUS COMMERCIAL

Manufacturers meet the market for compact tractors with two distinct classes of equipment: residential or consumer products and commercial machines that have different specifications and are designed for extended hours of use and heavy-duty work. This distinction has a strong bearing on machine selection, matching, use, and cost. Keep these two product classes in mind as you read this chapter and when you scrutinize tractors.

SELECTION

The five Ps (price, power, parts, performance, and prestige) are key factors in selecting a compact tractor or riding mower. The particular order of these priorities depends mainly on who is buying, and buyers fall into several categories, such as professionals and landholders, who may or may not use their equipment for income-generating purposes.

New Holland isn't hesitant about the prestige value of certain tractors. CNH's Boomer TC 24 is shown here. CNH

Compact tractor performance and utility rank high on selection criteria. This New Holland TC Boomer with FEL and belly mower makes a versatile combination. CNH

Retirees often have more discretionary spending power, and small tractors look highly appealing on their estates, acreage, or hobby farms. At the same time, retirees and urbanites may not be equipment savvy. They may not care to go to a farm machinery dealership to shop for their compact tractor or riding mower. Mass merchandisers are convenient places to shop, but they don't provide technical advice or service. The need for servicing the machine may not even enter the unwary

buyer's mind. Here's a brief review of those five machine selection priorities.

Price

The retail price of new tractors ranges from $250 to $1,000 per horsepower, which is such a wide range that it's not a lot of help in and of itself. What counts is value for money. To achieve that, the key is to be well informed before you buy. At the very least you need to investigate model year and release timing, resale value, package pricing, service and spare parts availability, and financing. Some less-obvious costs of tractor ownership are covered in more detail in Chapter 10. The cheap machines may not have the service backup with what is available for the more expensive machines. Mass-merchandisers may offer the cheapest option, but they do not provide any service backup. The dealerships of reputable manufacturers will stand behind their brands and take care of warrantees, even if their models are bought from a mass merchandiser.

Power

How much power your tractor requires depends on the tasks it will perform (see Chapter 3 for further information). There are advantages to buying a bit more power than anticipated. The machine will cost more, but it should last longer and will definitely provide greater satisfaction in the long run. Frustrations arise when a lower-powered tractor proves too slow for the task, you find there are more things to do than originally expected of the tractor, or the smaller tractor is inadequate and underpowered for some of the jobs. On the other hand, a more powerful tractor will probably be larger and take up more shed space, be less agile, and will cost more to operate.

Parts

Availability of parts and service is very important for professional users. Difficulty in getting parts or service in the event of a breakdown is frustrating for any owner, so definitely take parts availability into consideration to minimize downtime. Be especially wary of gray market tractors (see Chapter 10) because some parts may never be available in the United States.

Gianni Ferrari of Italian racing fame offers a prestige range of specialist compact tractors in the United States. Ferrari

The options and variations on a theme are abundant as seen in this collection of New Holland Boomer TC DA series models. CNH

This quick and handy tractor matching chart gives some notional values of power needed for several types of jobs. Check with the manufacturer's specifications or dealer for more specifics.

PTO power, horsepower	Mower, Rotary Finishing, feet	Slasher, Mounted or Trailed, feet	FEL Bucket Width (feet); Breakout (pounds)	3PL Lift—24-inch 3PL Lift—24-inch	Rotary Hoe Size, feet
10 to 25	4 to 7	4 or 5	4; 950	700 to 2,000	2 to 4
25 to 40	5 to 9	5 to 8	5; 1,800	2,200	4 to 6
40 to 55	8 to 16	8 to 15	7; 3,500	3,000	5 to 7
55 to 75	Up to 21	13 to 20	7; >3,500	3,300	6 to 10

Performance

Performance involves such things as engine torque rise, gear range, PTOs, implement linkages, hydraulic output, and field capacity. Tractor reliability must also be considered because it affects machine downtime, and that is directly related to performance. Performance is covered more in detail in Chapter 8.

Prestige

This may be hard to quantify, but certainly some products look better or are superior to others. Appearances are vital when it comes to trading in your tractor. Did you know there are tractor models available from the world's most prestigious racing car stables, including Lamborghini and Ferrari. Bragging rights, anyone?

TRACTOR WORK RATES

Matching tractor size to the task and the acreage is an important thing to remember when selecting a tractor. A ride-on mower will be a good match if it's confined to mowing grass on a small, level yard. Much depends on the lay of the land or landscape. On the other hand, if you want to plow a field, bale hay, pull stumps, move earth, and generally use a range of attachments, a more powerful machine with ground clearance is required.

Don't expect a model built for the consumer-product market and intended for a low amount of hours a year and lighter duties to hack the heavy stuff. Commercial machines cost more because they are built for higher hours of use and heavy-duty work. The distinction applies to both compact tractors and their attachments or implements. Chapter 7 explores this in more detail.

Selecting a Mower

There are several categories of mowers depending on what sort of finish is required. Rough slashing, shredding, mulching, topping, or brush hogging usually involves uneven terrain and needs more underframe clearance than ride-on mowers provide. Allow roughly 4 to 7 tractor PTO horsepower per foot of cut depending on how heavy the growth. For example, an 18- PTO-horsepower diesel FWA can cope with a 4-foot cutting deck. Self-powered trailed mowers (pulled behind or to the side) are a valuable alternative for knocking down rough grass and weeds. They also help widen your cutting swath and speed up the job when used in conjunction with a tractor-mounted mower. They are made with their own support/depth wheels and an engine mounted on the frame. A 5-foot trailed unit may have 11 to 15 horsepower on board, which has less power than a mowing tractor because it doesn't have to move itself. More information on this is available in Chapter 5.

Blade and Box-Scraper Work

Allow 5 to 6 PTO horsepower per foot of blade width, depending on soil conditions. For example an 18-horsepower diesel can handle a 4-foot box scraper, a 5-foot front blade, 5-foot rotary broom, and a 6-foot landscape rear rake, but not all at once!

Light Cultivation and Digging

Mini-loaders are on their own when it comes to speedy, small-scale earthmoving. On the other hand, the versatile tractor front-end loader (FEL) can be used with digger teeth (installed on the bucket frame) or reversible front blades designed for the task. Light-duty ripper teeth that loosen the soil facilitate bucket and scraper work. Allow about 7 horsepower per foot of cultivator width.

Kubota models B2630 and B3030 showing TLB and ROPS, bare FWA tractor with ROPS and grille guard, and full-cab and midmount mower options. Kubota

Moving Snow

Snow removal can be slippery work. A mounted snow thrower is best for deep drifts and may have its own engine. Wheel weights for traction and tire chains are necessary for serious snow plowing, which can be done with either a loader bucket, a purpose-built snowplow, front- or rear-mounted blades, or a snow blower. Allow roughly 5 horsepower per foot of blade width.

DECISIONS

Let's take a stroll around the machine and build a virtual tractor! The general principles will apply, whether it's a ride-on mower, mowing tractor, skid-steer loader, zero-turn, or utility work vehicle. Here's a sequential approach.

The first decision to make is about the tractor's power range, which depends on the job and the attachments you select to do the job. Be as specific as possible about what you need to do with the tractor, now and for the next five years. Now for the details:

Engine Type, Power, and Fuel

In the trade literature you will find several engine ratings specified, which are explained in detail in Chapter 3. Power take-off (PTO) horsepower at rated engine speed is the more useful number for matching to the job. Fueling the tractor will often be governed by what else you have in the yard. Do you stock your own fuel in bulk or fill containers at the gas station? Do you want to have just one type of fuel for your auto, mowers, and portables and therefore stay with that for your tractor as well?

Ground Drive

Wheels or tracks? Two-wheel drives (2WD) have the drawback of having to push a pair of nontraction wheels. Four-wheel drives (4WD) or front-wheel assists (FWA) have powered front axles and cost more, but are superior in all conditions, especially in soft ground and rough going.

Tires

There are many tire types to choose from, including traction grip-type, turf, and all-terrain. Your main determinant is what kind of terrain are you driving over.

Transmission Type

Hydrostatic transmissions are the simplest to operate, with no more than a range lever or foot pedal with instant reversing, but they can hinder power and gas mileage. Manual

MTD's Cub Cadet 7000 series has independent live 540-rpm rear PTO and 2,000-rpm mid-PTO for midmount equipment. MTD Products

A fully enclosed, air-conditioned cab environment makes driving this Kubota B3030 tractor fun while mowing. Kubota

CASE STUDY

Mow an acreage with a 6-foot-wide, belly-mount mower under a compact tractor at an average speed of 5 miles per hour and 80 percent field efficiency. An operator with that machine at that rate will cover 2.9 acres an hour (actual field capacity = theoretical field capacity x 0.80). When the overall acreage to be covered is known, you have to decide how much time you will allow for the job. For example, if you have 12 acres to mow with a 6-foot deck machine, then it will take 12 ÷ 2.9, which rounds off at 4 hours of work (time in hours = total area in acres ÷ actual field capacity in acres per hour).

CHECKLIST

This is a 10-point checklist to help you define your needs and select a compact tractor. Complete this before you go shopping for a compact tractor.

1. How much are you prepared to spend on the tractor and its equipment?
2. What's the absolute upper price limit?
3. What's the main task for the tractor?
4. If it is used for mowing or fieldwork, how many acres will it involve?
5. How many hours a day do you anticipate using the tractor?
6. How many hours a year will you clock on the tractor?
7. Who is the dealer and what service does it provide?
8. How far away is the dealership from your home?
9. Is ground clearance a consideration?
10. Do you need a full cab?

Attachments and Accessories

What accessories do you think you will need?

Alternative Course of Action

You may consider alternatives to buying, such as leasing, renting, or hiring a contractor. If your decision is to buy a tractor, will it be new or used? This aspect is covered in more detail in Chapter 11.

The time it takes to mow an acre with this tractor and mower is greatly reduced. AGCO

shift transmission is more economical, but more complicated. An option for front-end loader-equipped tractors with mechanical transmissions is shuttle shift that gives instant forward-to-reverse electronically through the gears where there is a lot of back-and-forth work. Riding mowers in the lower power range have several other transmission choices, such as variable speed belt and cone-friction drives.

PTO Speeds

There are several PTO options for compacts. The 1,000-rpm PTO can transmit more power than the 540-rpm PTO. The 1,000- and 2,000-rpm PTOs are also valuable for faster-driven equipment such as fire-fighting pumps or hydraulic power packs.

Brakes and Differential Lock

The difflock is almost universal today on the better tractor models. The difference between wet and dry brakes is dry brakes have the brake assemblies outside the transmission and are more readily accessed for maintenance. Wet brakes are built into the transmission housing and tend to be more durable.

It is time to mow an acre with different finishing mowers from a small hand-push type or walker to a sophisticated self-propelled three-gang machine cutting a 7-foot swath (see Chapter 10 for details).

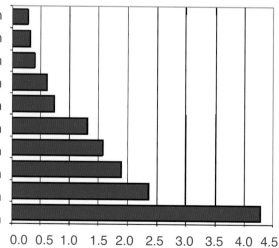

Above and next page: You may be proud to have this machine parked on your lot, but are the owning and operating costs justifiable? If it's a job you don't have to do too often, would you save by bringing in a contractor, renting, or leasing? See Chapter 9 for more information. Kubota

Operator's Platform

There are two different options in this category. The straddle type is the one with the transmission hump between the operator's legs. Step-through platforms have an uncluttered flat floor space for easy access from either side.

Cab

A rollover protection system (ROPS) is mandatory on bigger compacts with no cab and is highly desirable on any tractor. An extended two-post ROPS with a cantilevered top or a four-post ROPS are useful for additional protection and can also carry a sunshade. An enclosed cab is the ultimate in comfort. A noise-deadening cab contributes to increased machine-operator productivity by reducing fatigue, giving protection from the elements, providing radio/CD entertainment, and reducing the number of breaks an operator may take during the workday.

PTO Alternatives

Rear-, mid-, and front-mounted PTOs are available as possibilities. See Chapter 4 for more information.

Drawbar and/or Three-Point—or Other—Linkage (3PL)

Three-point hitches can be mounted on the front or rear. It also depends on what draft/depth control you need for your three-point hitch.

Remote Hydraulics and Valve Stack

If you plan to use implements that have hydraulic actuators, such as cylinders and hydraulic motors, then you need to check out remote hydraulics, which can come with one to four remote outlets and separate control valves.

Wheel Ballast or Saddle Weights

A tractor performs best when the machine is appropriately ballasted for a certain front-to-rear axle weight distribution, dictated by whether there is a lot of drawbar work or if there is an FEL up front, etc. Weight can be applied at the front or rear of the tractor.

Lights

Headlights, taillights, and turn indicators are important if you will be driving at night or on public roads. If driving on public roadways it's essential to fit a slow-moving vehicle (SMV) emblem on the back of the tractor.

Buddy Seat

Some tractor platforms have a passenger seat. A seat belt must be used with the buddy seat. If there is no passenger seat, under no circumstances should riders accompany the driver.

Extra Steer Functions

Skid steers aside, some situations are better handled with a tractor equipped with extra-sharp turning capability. The tighter the turn, the narrower the headland when working a field. New Holland has tractor models with SuperSteer where the whole front axle pivots a few degrees to tighten the turning radius. FWA tractors can turn much sharper than the traditional 2WD tractor configuration. Kubota goes a different way with an automatic speed-up powered front axle when turning sharply on some tractor models.

Grille Guards

A protective guard on the tractor grille is valuable to protect the front of the tractor against mishaps, especially working near trees or with front-end loaders. Preserving the appearance of the tractor, such as the tinwork at the front, the grille, and the radiator, is well worth it when it comes to trade-in time.

WHAT ATTACHMENTS ARE AVAILABLE FOR COMPACT TRACTORS?

The categories of equipment are wide and the range within categories is extensive. Some of the more common attachments used are mowers, front-end loaders with a range of buckets and accessories, backhoes, rotary hoes and a range of tillage equipment, blades, rakes, sweepers, snowplows and blowers, sprayers, and generators. Seek help and use common sense in the decision making. There are websites with loads of information. Resources can be found at dealerships and public extension agencies. See Chapter 7 for further information.

If you are definitely going to buy a compact tractor, there are four steps to keep in mind.

Step 1. Clearly have in mind the requirements for the machine.

Step 2. Determine which attachments are needed before deciding on the tractor or power unit.

Step 3. Match the correct power unit, including the power needed for any attachments, to the job.

Step 4. Budget what you are prepared to pay for the machine or the overall job. Budgeting should involve calculating what things cost to own and operate. Choose the most economical route. It may be cheaper to rent a machine or hire a contractor than to own and operate the set of equipment yourself because there are always hidden costs to owning.

This is an example of defining machine requirements.

If a lawn area has to be mowed, there is a simple way to figure the capacity and how big the equipment needs to be to accomplish the task.

Operating width of the mower machine in feet = 8.25 x acres per hour ÷ speed (miles per hour).

Alternatively, field capacity (in acres per hour) = machine width (feet) x average speed (miles per hour) ÷ 8.25.

These are theoretical values, and in practice the actual rates of work are reduced by a factor called field efficiency (FE). For example, with a fairway mowing job, FE = 0.7 (or 70 percent efficiency) because of the amount of maneuvering time, equipment overlap on each pass, operator, and other delays. This is covered in more detail in Chapter 8.

CHAPTER 3
POWER AND ENGINES: HOW MUCH POWER IS ENOUGH?

ENGINE PERFORMANCE

The engine is the heart and pulse of a tractor, but how is the heart's performance measured? System productivity or work capability is closely associated with engine power. Power is the rate of doing work in a given time. Work in linear movement is measured by multiplying force by distance. Power is the time/rate at which work is done.

Horsepower is the critical measure of an engine. Tractor literature will specify at least two and often three horsepower figures. One figure is gross engine horsepower, which is defined under Standard J1995 by the Society of Automotive Engineers (SAE) as the power output of the engine tested bare (without accessories, mufflers, or emission control devices) on a dynamometer test stand. The test reflects a

This is one of AGCO's ST Series compact tractors with 3PL box scraper. AGCO

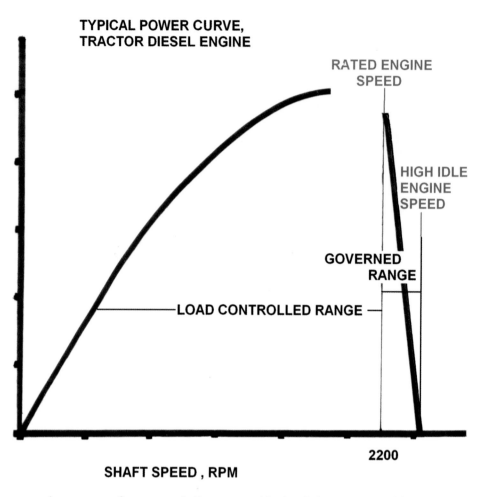

TYPICAL POWER CURVE, TRACTOR DIESEL ENGINE

RATED ENGINE SPEED

HIGH IDLE ENGINE SPEED

GOVERNED RANGE

LOAD CONTROLLED RANGE

2200

SHAFT SPEED , RPM

This characteristic engine power curve over the full speed range shows rated and high idle speeds. Also shown are governed and load-controlled ranges.

maximum or theoretical value, not the power, of an installed engine. The engine is not attached to the clutch or transmission or any of the normal tractor functional components like the steering pump, but it does include driving the fan and alternator or whatever parts are necessary to make the engine run. On the other hand, the literature will often also quote SAE net horsepower, which is defined by Standard J1349 and reflects the rated flywheel power of the engine in as-installed trim with all accessories plus standard intake and exhaust systems. To be truly meaningful, any power rating must always be accompanied by the engine speed at which that power was measured; manufacturers specify a rated engine speed.

Since August 2004, a new standard has been adopted in order to tighten some minor loopholes or ambiguities that existed in J1349. The SAE certified horsepower is defined in a new test procedure for monitoring engine torque and horsepower. This test is voluntary, but there must be an independent certifying officer present to scrutinize the tests. Engines completing tests under Procedure J2723 can be advertised as "SAE certified." This designation will show up eventually in compact-tractor

trade literature and is already in some reputable automotive trade publication.

ENGINE DISPLACEMENT

Right up there with the specs on any tractor brochure will be engine displacement. It's the volumetric capacity inside the engine and is determined by the engine cylinder-bore area multiplied by stroke length multiplied by number of cylinders. Displacement = $0.785B2 \times S \times n$; where displacement will be in cubic inches when cylinder bore size B and stroke length S are in inches, and n is the number of cylinders. Note that displacement is a measure of the bulkiness of the engine, it is not an accurate guide to power.

PTO POWER

The next tractor power spec after engine power is PTO power, which is the tractor's output measured by coupling the machine to the dynamometer through the PTO shaft. The PTO horsepower is always less than gross or net power because of the ancillaries driven by the engine plus some drive components in between that detract from gross power. For example, the popular 23-horsepower John

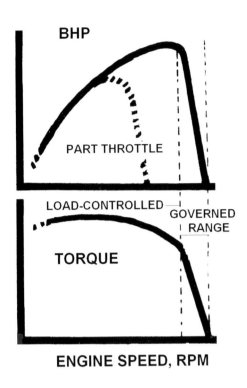

Engine power and torque curves and speed showing governed and load-controlled ranges.

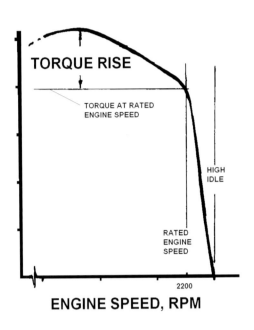

This torque curve shows torque rise as the engine is pulled down below rated speed by the load giving an engine lugging ability.

Deere model 2210 compact tractor has a 1 liter or 61.4-ci engine, gross SAE power of 23 horsepower, and a PTO power of 17.7 horsepower, all at 3,000-rpm rated engine speed. Some documents, such as Nebraska Tractor Test Laboratory reports, specify drawbar power, which is power available at the drawbar to pull equipment. Drawbar power will be less than PTO power because of losses through the transmission, final drives, and from wheels-to-ground or tractive system losses. Drawbar power measured in one place is extremely difficult to replicate somewhere else. Nebraska standardizes drawbar tests by pulling the load car dynamometer on a paved surface.

RATED ENGINE SPEED VERSUS HIGH IDLE SPEED

All compact tractor engines have a governor that, regardless of load, attempts to maintain the speed set by the operator's throttle setting. When the torque load exceeds the governor's maximum, the engine's speed will be out of the governed range and controlled by the load. The rated speed is usually the engine speed the manufacturer deems suited to the tractor application. It is slightly lower than high idle speed and represents that speed where the load is about to take over from the governor. Maximum horsepower is usually, but not always, found at rated speed. The expression

"power bulge" is found in some trade literature and refers to engines tuned to increase power slightly when pulled below rated speed. A common rated engine speed for bigger diesel tractors is 2,200 rpm. High idle for that same engine might be, say, 2,300 rpm. Gasoline-powered tractor engines may have rated speeds of 3,500 to 4,500 rpm. Rated engine speed is the speed where the governor is about to hand over to the load. High idle speed is a no-load speed. It's a few percent higher than rated speed, and in one sense it is an indicator of the accuracy of the governor. There is absolutely no benefit in having a worn governor because they are power robbers when it comes to fieldwork. Electric gensets particularly need tight governor control within 1 percent of rated speed. Tractor governors hold speed to within 2 to 5 percent of rated engine speed.

TORQUE

Torque is the output shaft's twisting or turning effort and measured in foot-pounds. Torque multiplied by the shaft's rotational speed calculates shaft power as follows: Shaft horsepower = torque (ft-lbs) x N (rpm) ÷ 5,252.

The engine speed for peak torque is usually lower than the rated engine speed. The speed difference will be more than 30 percent for diesels.

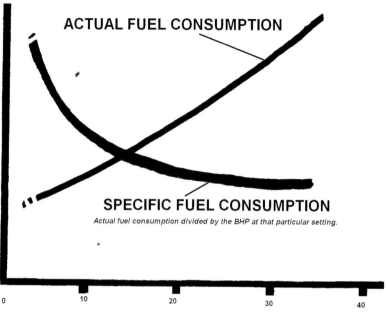

ACTUAL FUEL CONSUMPTION

SPECIFIC FUEL CONSUMPTION

Actual fuel consumption divided by the BHP at that particular setting.

Actual fuel consumption increases with power demand from an engine, but SFC is an entirely different story. The SFC curve traces out a hyperbolic function.

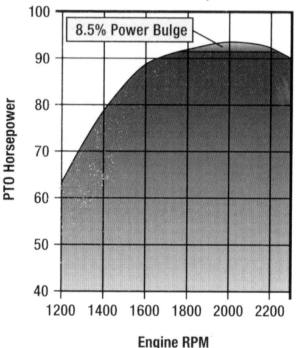

It comes down to horsepower versus rpm curve of a tractor engine that has power bulge. This Deere 6420's breakdown is 8.5 percent.

DIESEL OR GASOLINE?

Tractors use two main types of engines: Diesel engines ignite the injected fuel by means of the heat generated in the combustion chamber by high compression of the induced air. Diesels are heavier, a bit noisier and more expensive, but the engine is far more durable and economical to operate than a spark-ignited engine of similar horsepower (especially when idling) and has highly desirable torque characteristics for tractor work. A well-maintained

diesel tractor can be expected to have a working life up to 12,000 hours, which is much longer than a gasoline-powered unit. Gasoline engines are still the predominant type for low-end markets, lower-powered machines, and lightweight applications such as ride-ons and portable equipment. Diesel fuel has a higher flash point so it's safer to store, but fuel cleanliness is critical. Don't store diesel fuel too long and be aware that there are summer and winter grades. Keep diesel clean and separate from other fuels. With tax breaks, there are price differences between diesel used commercially, as in farming, versus private use. Gasoline-powered tractors need an ignition system, similar to your car or truck (unless you have a diesel-powered auto), and have some advantages if you don't want to store two kinds of fuel. There are some spark-ignited engines that are simple enough to do your own engine repairs.

LUGGING ABILITY

Diesel engines have lugging ability, which means they can maintain a steady or rising level of torque and hang in there under load even when the engine has slowed down considerably—to two-thirds of its rated speed. Lugging ability has a lot to do with the engine's induction system, valves, and cylinder head design.

TORQUE RISE

Torque rise may range from 5 to 45 percent and is essential out in the field to prevent the machine from stalling or needing a gear change when the tractor encounters a slope or tougher working conditions. With torque reserve you

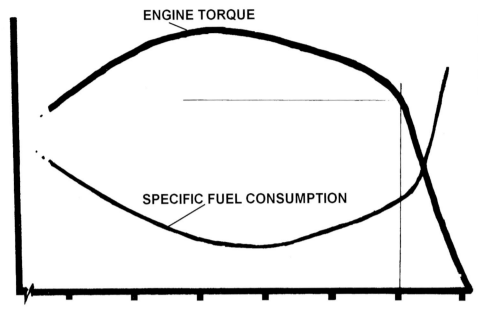

ENGINE TORQUE

SPECIFIC FUEL CONSUMPTION

ENGINE SPEED, RPM

These are characteristic SFC curves for a diesel engine. Note that the most efficient point is at a similar speed to the peak torque speed for this engine. Fuel efficiency is poor at high idle.

can keep going without changing gears, even if the engine is slowed to two-thirds of its rated speed. In practical terms, the diesel's superior lugging ability means that a tractor with a spark-ignited engine would need to be somewhat more powerful to do the job than a diesel.

FUEL ECONOMY

Engines deliver only 40 percent or less of the power latent in the fuel. A lot of the wasted energy goes out the exhaust stack and through the engine cooling system. Fuel economy, measured only as gallons an hour, is not highly relevant, but what is more meaningful is how much work can the tractor deliver in the hour with that gallon. Test authorities measure specific fuel consumption (SFC) which is an inverse indicator of the engine efficiency. The lower the SFC means the higher the thermal efficiency will be. The units of SFC are gallons per hour horsepower (gal/hp/h).

While your immediate running expense is more concerned with the gallons per hour that the engine burns, SFC really is what counts in a professional setting. A tractor that uses very little fuel might only be good for pulling a broom. Note that tractors operate most efficiently in terms of horsepower output per unit of fuel input (gal/h/hp) at around the same speed as peak torque. Thus for fuel economy, operate the tractor at that speed (say two-thirds of its rated engine speed for a diesel) by gearing up and throttling back. Preserve engine and transmission life by operating somewhat faster and periodically varying the load.

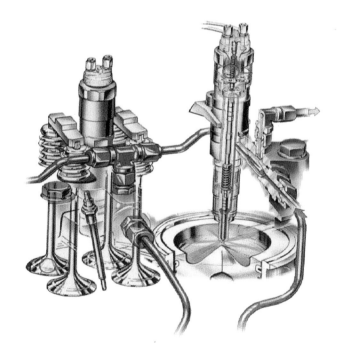

Deere's 6020 Series tractors (65 to 90 horsepower) are equipped with common rail injection. The fuel pump operates independent of engine speed to build up fuel pressure that is accumulated by the common-rail unit to supply each injector with constant high injection pressure. As a result, precise amounts of fuel are delivered even at low engine rpm. Deere Bulletin DSAA 11551

WEIGHT-TO-POWER RATIO

zmercial) is around 88 pounds of tractor shipping weight per PTO horsepower. The range is around 65 to 110 pounds/PTO horsepower. The hydrostatic transmission

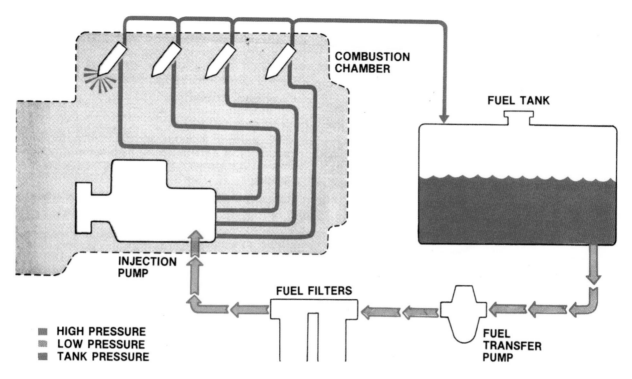

This is a typical diesel fuel system. Clean fuel is critical for reliable engine performance. Deere FMO

tractors are in the 100-plus area and the mechanicals are at the lower end of the weight-to-power range. Consumer compact tractors usually don't power through the PTO, so net horsepower is used, but in any case, the ratio comes down to the 27 to 40 pounds/net horsepower range.

NOISE

The noise level at the height of the operator's ear is something to check when buying a tractor. There are very definite hazards associated with excess noise exposure (for more detail, see Chapter 9). It's not uncommon for older tractors to emit a deafening 100 dBa at full load. Modern tractors have been cut back to a comfortable 73 dBa inside the cab.

EMISSIONS

Tougher standards on vehicle emissions are emerging regularly and manufacturers strive to meet or exceed those standards. The emission standards apply equally to tractors and automobiles. The standards deal with particulate emissions, carbon monoxide, and oxides of nitrogen, which are all products of combustion. Modern diesels, particularly two-stroke engines, have come a long way with electronic fuel injection and stratified-charge systems respectively, to be able to exceed current California Air Resources Board (CARB) and Environmental Protection Agency (EPA) standards.

DIESEL INJECTION–COMMON RAIL AND OTHER INJECTION

There are three general systems of mechanical diesel-fuel injection: the constant pressure or common-rail system, the spring pressure or accumulator type, and the jerk pump. Most compact tractors still use the jerk-type fuel-injection system but the common rail is rapidly moving in. The common rail was first commercialized on automotive diesels, and then moved into the bigger tractors. The advantages of common-rail injection are a cleaner-burning system with lower emissions, a more responsive engine, and higher thermal efficiency (more horsepower per gallon per hour = lower SFC). Look for common-rail injection to appear on compact tractors in the near future.

A FURTHER WORD ABOUT FUELS

When fueling your tractor, make sure no dirt or moisture gets into the tank. It is best to fill the tank at the end of each workday to minimize condensation. Be aware that there are two grades of diesel, summer and winter. Avoid using summer-grade diesel in the winter because it could gel and block your fuel system. Whatever the situation, avoid keeping diesel fuel for more than six months and monitor storages for moisture and contaminants. The latest renewable fuels, such as ethanol blends and biodiesel, bring another set of cautions. Follow the tractor manufacturer's instructions before filling up on those fuels. Fuel stabilizing additives are

worthwhile if that fuel has to be stored over winter. Additives prolong the life of the fuel system and filters, improve starting, and enhance engine performance.

TURBOS

Modern tractor diesel engines, even down to 20 horsepower, can be sold with turbochargers. That results in massive improvements in power output and fuel efficiency compared with their naturally aspirated kin. Turbos allow a smaller engine envelope in a more powerful tractor. Bigger farm tractors are often also equipped with induction aftercooling for even better diesel efficiency.

AIR COOLING VERSUS LIQUID COOLING

A great advantage of air-cooled engines is that they are lighter. There is no radiator or need for water, which immediately eliminates freezing problems in winter. On the other hand, air-cooled engines are noisier and dust buildup problems can occur in extremes. Antifreeze additives take care of winter problems if liquid-cooled engines are properly maintained.

TWO-STROKE VERSUS FOUR-STROKE

Two-stroke engines, which are widely used in portable equipment, including chain saws, are uncommon in compact tractors. Two-strokes are usually lightweight and compact compared to four-strokes of similar displacement. They tend to be less durable and are not intended for continuous heavy-duty applications.

HORIZONTAL CRANKSHAFT VERSUS VERTICAL CRANKSHAFT

Vertical-shaft engines are useful for belly-mount riding mower applications where a direct belt drive from the engine powers the blades. The more widely used horizontal-shaft engines require a more complicated drive system to get down to the cutters. On the other hand, horizontal-shaft engine configurations are better suited and somewhat easier to service on modern tractors with multiple PTOs, hydrostatics, and other functions.

SINGLE CYLINDER VERSUS MULTICYLINDER

Multicylinder engines are obviously more complex, but if you need a powerful tractor, multicylinder engines have less vibration and run smoothly.

HOW MUCH POWER IS ENOUGH?

It is common for tractor owners to find that they don't have as much power as they would like. There are many reasons, such as the tractor is too slow, there are more jobs than originally expected of the tractor, or the smaller tractor is underpowered for some jobs. Buying a bit more power than anticipated will cost more, but the machine should last longer and prove more versatile. Weigh that up against the more powerful tractor being larger, taking up more room, being less agile, and costing more to operate.

CHAPTER 4
TRANSMITTING POWER

HARNESSING THE HORSES: TRACTOR POWER OUTLETS

Tractor engines are tested on a dynamometer at the factory. Reputable manufacturers also have some tractor models formally tested by an independent test agency and the engines are given a flywheel power rating. When you see engine power on trade literature, it's usually the flywheel power of the bare engine at the manufacturer's rated engine speed and is power available for doing useful work. The several horsepower ratings are outlined in Chapter 3.

To turn flywheel power into useful effort at the drawbar or elsewhere requires a drivetrain and transmission to bring the speed down to the respective outlets, such as the PTO and drive wheels. Many of the tractor-driven attachments, such as mowers, need to be operated at a constant speed usually at or near full throttle. The function of the

Above and opposite: New Holland's SuperSteer system can complete tight turns with Ackermann-steered front wheels and pivoting axle. SuperSteer cuts the turning diameter by 50 percent. CNH

transmission is to allow the tractor's motion to be varied while maintaining a constant engine speed for the driven attachments. The drive wheels on a typical compact tractor only revolve at 145 rpm in road gear, so there is quite a reduction (16 to 1) needed from an engine running at 2,300 rpm to get down to the final-drive axles.

PTO power is less than flywheel power due to losses in the drivetrain to the PTO. The power from the PTO may be 82 to 90 percent of engine power with the PTO shaft speed having been geared down from the engine by one-third or more.

Drawbar power is rarely listed because traction conditions are so variable that rendering such a rating is virtually unrepeatable in practice and in any case is even harder for users to verify.

Power steering is frequently available on tractors, even on small garden tractors and riding mowers. For constant use, such as commercial mowing, especially with tractors

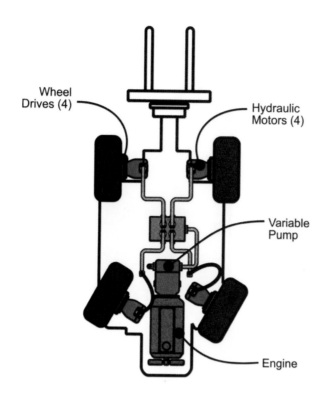

Wheel Drives (4)

Hydraulic Motors (4)

Variable Pump

Engine

HST Transmission schematic. Vickers Mobile Hydraulics Manual

clutch, but they cost more initially than a manual transmission. Hydros are heavier, take more internal power, and will raise your tractor's fuel bill by 10 to 20 percent. They have several big advantages over straight mechanical transmissions, namely the extreme simplicity to drive, they have a lower risk of damage to the tractor, a smooth adaptation or matching of load to speed, and they are amenable to electronic management systems. Hydros are continuously or infinitely variable transmissions (CVTs or IVTs, which, in large tractors can include units with a combination of mechanical and hydrointegrated transmissions in the one casing). Hydros use an engine-driven hydraulic pump or pumps to supply oil under pressure to a hydraulic motor or motors to turn the wheels. The displacement of the master pump is usually variable. It can be increased, decreased, or reversed to give the directionality and speed range. There's no clutch pedal to engage or gears to select which makes them easier to operate. They often have just one pedal that governs forward or reverse movement, as well as speed in either direction. An electronic cruise control is provided on some models for foot-free driving.

The hydraulic pump and motor combinations inside a hydrostatic drive generate more heat than a mechanical transmission and need a separate cooling system, which causes power loss and added complexity. An HST-equipped tractor may be offered with a slightly more powerful engine than its mechanical sister. Hydrostatic transmissions need extreme care to avoid any contamination of the hydraulic fluid, which performs several important functions including

that are heavily loaded on the front wheels, power steering is an arm saver. For intermittent use, some owners may prefer the lower cost of a manually steered tractor. When the turns are really tight, the differential brakes (independent brakes for each rear wheel, which ought to be locked together for over-the-road use) greatly tighten turns. One drawback of power steering on smaller tractors is that the tractor can be slower to warm up in the winter. Once you've driven a tractor with power steering, it's unlikely you will ever be without it!

New Holland's Boomer series and several other models offer an optional sharp-turn feature they call SuperSteer. This allows the front axle as well as the wheels to swivel wagonlike for a few degrees, for a 40 percent tighter turn.

Kubota's Bi-Speed steering system rotates the wheels faster at nearly twice the peripheral speed of the rear wheels when the front wheel turns at more than about 35 degrees. The result is a smoother, tighter turn.

HYDROSTATIC TRANSMISSIONS

Hydrostatic transmissions (HSTs), often called hydrodrives, are becoming increasingly popular. HSTs don't need a

Toro's TimeCutter zero-turn mower has a wide deck. Toro

Each rear drive wheel of the Dixon ZTR garden tractor has its own closed-center HST transmission with integrated hydraulic pump and motor. Dixon

transmitting power to the motors or other linear rotary actuators, cooling the system by dissipating heat throughout the reservoir and cooling devices, lubricating sliding or rotating surfaces, and carrying contaminants to filters and the reservoir.

Hydrostatic transmissions, being clutchless and often controlled by just one lever or pedal, make maneuvering any mobile equipment much easier. HSTs come standard on many models. A majority of skid-steer loaders are hydrostatically propelled.

MECHANICAL TRANSMISSIONS

Smaller ride-on tractors, utility vehicles, and all-terrain vehicles (ATVs) also have continuously variable transmissions (CVTs), but they deploy a belt transmission. This type of transmission is the cheapest type of CVT, with a pair of split-sheaves and V-drive belt. As the belt rides higher or lower between the respective sheaves, the effective speed ratio changes. Variable-speed ratios are achieved by varying the pitch diameter of the driving sheave. The driven pulley is spring loaded so it moves opposite of the control sheave. When the speed control lever or pedal is moved, the

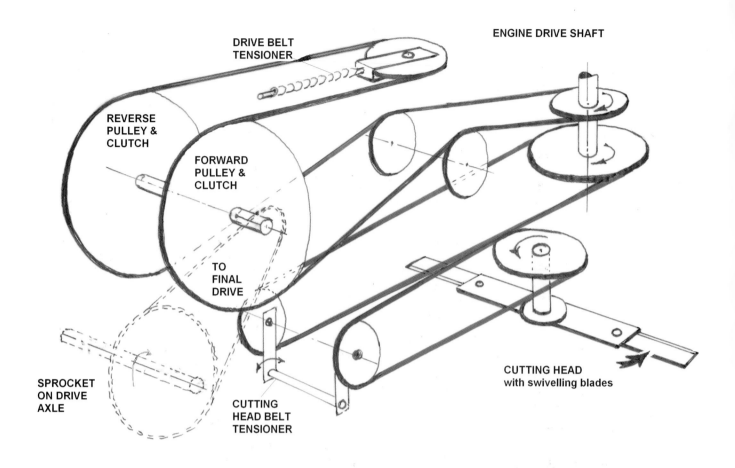

DRIVE BELT TENSIONER

ENGINE DRIVE SHAFT

REVERSE PULLEY & CLUTCH

FORWARD PULLEY & CLUTCH

TO FINAL DRIVE

SPROCKET ON DRIVE AXLE

CUTTING HEAD BELT TENSIONER

CUTTING HEAD
with swivelling blades

These are serpentine V-belt drives on a riding mower. The upper A-section drive belt powers a pair of pulley/clutches that control forward and reverse motion. The lower B-section belt drives the cutting head. While the smaller belts have limited power transmitting capability, the great advantages of belt drives are dust tolerance, quietness, simplicity, and low cost.

transmission ratio is effectively changed to control the tractor's motion. Belt drives are quiet, simple, and cheap, but they are limited in transmitting power up to 15 horsepower. This type of transmission is not used in heavier tractors because it doesn't have the torque ratings of the other transmissions. Belt drives are more for speedy vehicles that don't pull heavy loads and are not strictly for drawbar work.

There are a few ride-on tractor models that use friction-drive systems to provide similar performance to belts in the lower-power range. In one form, a movable cone-shaped friction element is pressed against the mating disc or cone to transfer power. Speed changes with belt or friction drives can only be changed while in motion.

The ideal situation is to have a gearbox that matches every load/speed combination. Mechanical transaxles are durable, but unless they are coupled with a variable-speed belt, they do not offer incremental speeds. A clutch pedal must be depressed before shifting gears. A popular low-cost, ride-on transmission uses a fixed-ratio belt drive into a three- to five-speed gearbox/transaxle. Using a belt drive

tensioned by an idler or by moving one pulley eliminates a friction clutch and the belt is slackened or tightened to provide clutching. The combination of a gear transmission with a variable-speed belt drive is low cost. The gears are still lever controlled for range shifting.

Mechanical transmissions will be around for a long time because most of the alternatives are less efficient and take more power and fuel. To accomplish something mechanically akin to a CVT, manufacturers are offering a large number of gears. On big tractors there can be as many as 24 forward speeds. On the compacts, the typical number is 8 to 12 forward speeds and 3 to 6 reverse gears. Many modern gearboxes have shuttle shift which allows almost seamless and foot-clutch-free gear changes at the flick of a switch or lever. Shuttle shift enables the operator to change from forward to reverse without having to bring the tractor to a complete stop. In some tractors, such as John Deere's SyncReverser transmission, shuttle shift applies irrespective of the range gear selected. The controller may also allow you to drive at a predetermined dial-in level of wheel slip. The

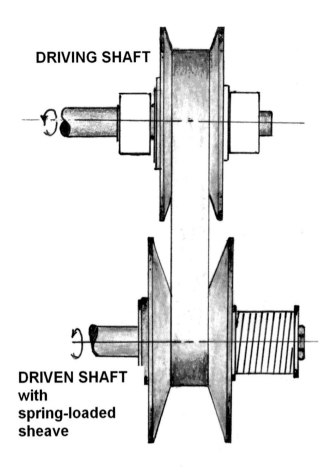

DRIVING SHAFT

DRIVEN SHAFT
with
spring-loaded
sheave

Variable-speed V-belt drive.

electronics do come at a price compared with the original and cheaper transmission or synchromesh gear transmissions.

DIFFERENTIALS

The outside wheels of conventional vehicles, including wheeled tractors, cut a wider arc than the inside wheels while cornering. A differential saves tire scrubbing on turns by allowing the respective wheels to turn at different speeds while still providing power through the drive axle. The problem is that the wheel with the least traction limits the net power. In the extreme case, if one wheel spins out, the tractor is immobilized.

LIMITED SLIP DIFFERENTIALS AND DIFFERENTIAL LOCK

A clutch pack incorporated into the differential casing enables a limited slip differential to share drive axle torque regardless of ground conditions. A differential lock is a mechanical device that provides power straight through the

axle to both wheels equally and effectively neutralizing the differential function by providing equal power to both wheels for better traction. Foot-pedal engagement of the tractor differential lock slides a collar or engages a clutch to tie the two drive axles together and is useful to quickly get through a boggy area or spot of loose soil. The differential lock automatically disengages when conditions return to normal and should never be used when turning or at speed. If for any reason the lock remains engaged after releasing the pedal, momentarily reduce drawbar load or apply a light braking load on the slipping rear wheel. The differential lock must not be used when turning.

2WD VERSUS 4WD AND FWA

A four-wheel-drive (4WD) tractor can do more work than a two-wheel-drive because it doesn't have to push a lazy (front) axle. With a 4WD you can scale back engine power for the same work capability, and a smaller 4WD tractor will be more maneuverable. Front-wheel assist (FWA) or mechanical front-wheel drive (MFWD) has swept across the market by providing 4WD in a more compact and cheaper envelope than a 4WD with equal-sized wheels. There are a subset of tractors specifically designed as a low-profile 4WD with equal-sized wheels, such as the Carraro and Ferrari tractor models, some with bidirectionality.

The FWA tractor, with its smaller rear wheels and traction front axle, can be safer to operate and will get you out of a difficult steering or mucky situation better than a 2WD. However on slopes, FWA can increase hazards because of the extra traction it provides. Many tractors allow the front-wheel drive to be disengaged on-the-go when it is not needed, such as traveling on roads at speed. There are ways to enhance traction with 2WD, including ballasting, tire chains, or equipping the tractor with more aggressive tire treads or duals.

ARTICULATED VERSUS FIXED CHASSIS

On rough ground, 4WD tractors with an articulated chassis allow each drive wheel to grip better than a tractor with a fixed frame. Models are offered with rear-axle steer, with or without oscillation, or all four wheels steerable. Some models have crab steering, which allows you to drive slightly sideways and is useful to keep the machine tracking straight ahead on hillsides.

TRACTION TO GROUND

Drive tires deliver power to the ground when pushed down by the weight on the axle. To get more pull out of a tractor, more weight is needed on the tire to achieve better contact with the soil and more grip. Tires for traction come in three

Dixon's Z drive transmits power by friction cone and plates. The company is using hydrostatic drives in response to demand. Dixon

principle types for compact tractors: The industry uses the code "R" for rear tires and an accompanying digit designates the tread type. Code "F" distinguishes front tires, which are usually ribbed, not lugged, if they are not powered. Tire sizes are indicated by a code for tire width and rim diameter. A 45-horsepower tractor with 18.4-28 rears has tires that are 18.4 inches wide on 28-inch-diameter rims. R-1 tires are bar or lugged agricultural tires for grip or traction with a regular chevron tread. R-2s are cane- and rice-field tires with deep treads. R-3 tires are shallow, nondirectional smooth treads designed for flotation and cause the least damage to the ground or a turf surface. R-4s are industrial tires with intermediate tread patterns for roadwork. R-4s are a compromise between the two tread-pattern extremes.

There are a number of other tire types for off-road and forestry use and rocky conditions. Radials are more expensive tires but they are popular because they have more flexible sidewalls and can be operated at lower pressure than

the traditional bias-ply tires. Radials have more contact with the ground, a softer ride, and reduced surface compaction. Since there is less wheel slip, radials achieve better tractor fuel economy.

Rubber tracks are an entirely different story. They are outstanding for low ground pressure, have high traction, and are puncture proof! A rubber-tracked tractor can have a traction efficiency (the capability of converting axle power into drawbar power) of 65 to 85 percent. Compare that with a 2WD tractor at 45 to 80 percent and a 4WD at 55 to 82 percent.

BALLASTING AND WEIGHT DISTRIBUTION

A tractor tire needs to have an appropriate amount of weight on it and correct tire pressure to get traction, prevent power hop, or in an extreme case, prevent rim slippage. For drawbar work, tractor weight needs to be matched to horsepower at a given working speed. For example, a 2WD tractor working at 4.5 miles per hour needs about 145

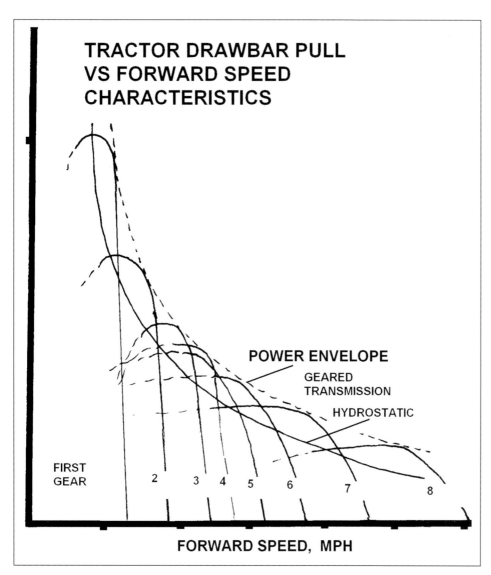

TRACTOR DRAWBAR PULL VS FORWARD SPEED CHARACTERISTICS

POWER ENVELOPE

GEARED TRANSMISSION

HYDROSTATIC

FIRST GEAR

2 3 4 5 6 7 8

FORWARD SPEED, MPH

This is a graph of HST versus geared transmission in the tractor power envelope context.

This is a tractor tire tread pattern. Note that the chevron "V" pattern should always point downwards at the front for traction. Occasionally this is reversed if the tractor will be doing a lot of road transport work or on the front axle of an FEL.

pounds/PTO horsepower. Generally, the static weight distribution for different styles of tractors should be as follows:

Style	Rear/Front
2WD	75/25 inches
4WD equal-sized wheels	40/60 inches
MFWD or FWA	60/40 inches

MECHANICALLY DRIVEN ATTACHMENTS

The simplest and cheapest way to drive an attachment is to use a belt-drive system. A belt drive provides built-in protection if the driven equipment, such as a mower cutting head, hits a rigid obstacle. The belt slips to protect the drivetrain and engine. Vertical-shaft engines in mowers are designed specifically to exploit the simplicity of a belt drive and take the power for the deck directly from the engine shaft and declutch the drive by belt slackening. Many ride-ons

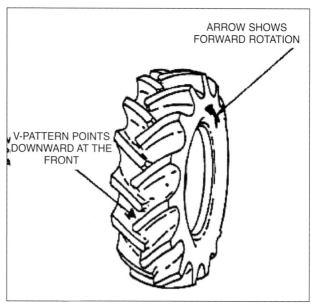

ARROW SHOWS FORWARD ROTATION

V-PATTERN POINTS DOWNWARD AT THE FRONT

49

A Bobcat S250 skid steer. Bobcat

today use an electrically operated clutch/brake instead of slipping the belt for engagement. When a switch on the tractor is moved, the clutch is engaged and the brake is disengaged; and vice versa when the switch is moved the other way. Straight-shaft drives are used on the larger, more expensive machines, but they need right-angle gearboxes and universal joints, which are more expensive. They can handle higher loads, such as big mower decks, but slip clutches are needed to protect the drivetrain against shock loads.

POWER TAKE-OFFS (PTOS)

Unlike pull-behind or trailed equipment—such as plows and cultivators—rotating machines need a PTO. For infrequent jobs like mulching prunings or powering a saw bench, the PTO on a compact tractor can save a lot of money by eliminating the need for separate engines. There are so many interesting pieces of equipment that can use the PTO. Fortunately, tractor designers in much of the world have standardized tractor PTOs so that tractor-driven

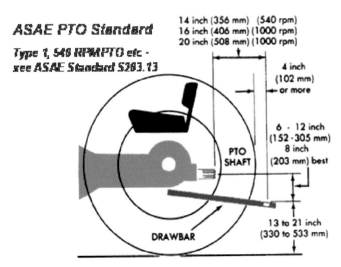

ASAE PTO Standard

**Type 1, 540 RPM PTO etc -
see ASAE Standard S203.13**

14 inch (356 mm) (540 rpm)
16 inch (406 mm) (1000 rpm)
20 inch (508 mm) (1000 rpm)

4 inch (102 mm) or more

6 - 12 inch (152 - 305 mm)
8 inch (203 mm) best

13 to 21 inch (330 to 533 mm)

PTO SHAFT

DRAWBAR

Geometry of ASAE PTO standards.

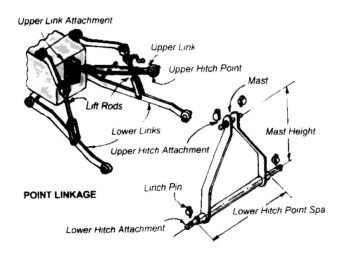

POINT LINKAGE

Upper Link Attachment
Upper Link
Upper Hitch Point
Mast
Lift Rods
Lower Links
Mast Height
Upper Hitch Attachment
Linch Pin
Lower Hitch Point Spa
Lower Hitch Attachment

Three-point-linkage components.

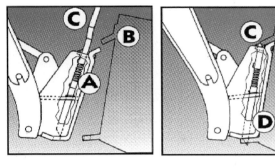

The PTO shield, which lifts up for access, and screw-on PTO cap are shown in the lower illustration. PTO shields must be kept in place at all times except during repair.

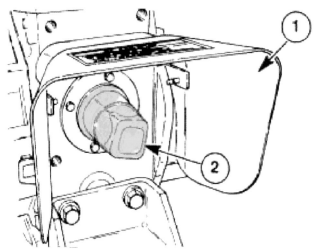

A range of John Deere and Frontier equipment is designed for rapid hitching with Deere's iMatch 3PL coupler system.

equipment or attachments can be readily interchanged between tractor makes. There are four standard mechanical-PTO-driveshaft types, depending on the tractor's power.

The original 540-rpm Type 1 PTO standard dates back to 1926 and is available for tractors up to 87 horsepower (65 kw). It uses a 1 3/8-inch shaft outside diameter with six splines. There are two 1,000-rpm Type 2 PTOs for tractors up to 160 horsepower (120 kw) with 1 3/8-inch, 21-tooth spline shaft. The Type 3 has a 20-spline, 1-3/4-inch shaft for power up to 255 horsepower (190 kw). The last version is the 2,000-rpm lawn and garden tractor PTO with a 1-inch, 15-tooth spline. The 2,000-rpm PTO is for tractors up to 27 horsepower (20 kw) and Category 0 linkage.

PTO POWER DELIVERY

Rear PTOs are located on back of the differential housing, but front- and mid-mount PTOs are available for the appropriate implements. There are several ways that the mechanical PTO power can be delivered to the splined output shaft. The transmission PTO operates only when the engine clutch is engaged. This means that the PTO stops or is interrupted when the master clutch is disengaged to stop tractor forward motion or change gears. The drawback with a transmission PTO is that if the tractor bogs down or loses traction, or if a rotary cutter or tiller jams, when you clutch to back up or engage four-wheel drive, the implement stops. It takes a while to get a rotary implement back up to full speed and you will lose time and momentum.

Continuous or live PTO has a two-stage clutch, which means the implement can continue running at normal speed when the tractor's forward motion stops. When the clutch is pushed halfway in, the main transmission is disengaged. When the clutch is fully depressed, the PTO and

Linkage Category	PTO power	horsepower at specified engine speed	Implement mast height inches/mm
0	Up to 27	Up to 20	12/305
I	Up to 64	Up to 48	18/457
II	Up to 123	Up to 92	19/483
III	107 to 248	80 to 185	22/559
IV	201 to 469	150 to 350	27/686

Table: ASAE Standards S217.12 and S919.
Notes: Speed in accordance with ISO 789-1. Detailed specifications of the linkages are found in the ASAE Standards. The 3PL lifting capability is related to drawbar power. For example, tractors with drawbar power up to 85 horsepower, the lift capacity must be at least 52 pounds per horsepower, so a 45-horsepower tractor should be able to lift at least 2,340 pounds at a distance of 24 inches behind the end of the lift links.

Avant articulated tractor with front mower. The rear axle articulates under the driver for steering. Avant

the main transmission are disengaged. The PTO cannot be engaged or disengaged unless the transmission is disengaged. Belly-mount mowers and front-mount accessories like snow blowers usually operate off special PTOs and are generally engaged with electric clutches. Also note that any stationary work with tractors, such as powering a chipper, saw bench, or a generator, does not need a live PTO.

Live independent PTO has its own clutch control, completely independent of the engine clutch and transmission. This method allows the PTO to be engaged and disengaged regardless of whether the tractor is moving or stationary. The PTO can continue to revolve while the tractor is stationary, or it can be engaged and disengaged while the tractor is in motion, which is not possible for the continuous-running PTO.

SAFETY

Most rear-PTO equipment is designed to operate at 540 rpm. The panel tachometer is marked to indicate 540 rpm, and if the needle registers above this mark, it represents a hazardous overspeed condition and the engine should be slowed immediately.

THREE-POINT-LINKAGE (3PL) CATEGORIES

Hydraulically raised linkages that permitted tractors to attach implements on the rear were standardized in 1959

This Kubota L30 is fitted with turf tires to minimize damage to greens. Kubota

(ASAE Standard S217.12). Today there are five categories of hitches, 0 through IV. The lightweight Category 0 lawn and garden tractor hitch equipment should be avoided in favor of a Category I hitch if the same implements are to be used with field-going tractors.

POWER THROUGH THE DRAWBAR; IMPLEMENT HITCHING

The drawbar is the usual way to pull an implement, but many attachments can be mounted under or elsewhere on the tractor frame with individual linkages adapted to that

attachment. Drawbars are either built into the tractor frame or can be attached to the 3PL. There is also the single-point, sleeve-hitch standard for small vehicles, but it is seldom used today. Rear drawbars may have a swinging arrangement to facilitate turning with heavier towed implements.

QUICK-ATTACH SYSTEMS

Hitches that permit rapid hitching without the operator leaving the tractor seat are available in various configurations. Bobcat's Bob-Tach and Deere's iMatch system are two examples.

This ASV loader can work in ground conditions that would be too difficult for tires, provided the operator doesn't turn sharply. Rubber tracks cause less surface disturbance in straight going and can be driven over a lawn without leaving wheel ruts. JCB Sales Limited

HYDRAULICALLY DRIVEN EQUIPMENT

Modern tractors are mobile hydraulic power packs! The engine is coupled to a hydraulic pump or series of pumps that include power steering, clutch actuation, hydrostatic drives, remote couplers, and linkage hydraulic pump. The hydraulic output is managed via valve sets (remotes) for actuators or ported direct via flexible hydraulic lines to hydraulic motors, such as the drives to hydraulic motors that rotate reel mowers, slashers, or harvesters. The great advantages of hydraulic drives are compactness and flexibility. In many cases, driveshafts, couplings, universal joints, belts, and gearboxes are eliminated. There are always some power losses through hydrostatics compared to mechanical drives, and the manufacturer has to provide additional cooling for the hydraulic fluid in these drives.

Many of the attachments, such as mower decks, need to operate at a constant speed, which is usually rated engine speed. This means varying the tractor's speed has to come from the transmission, not by varying the engine speed. Hydrostatic drive is the ultimate in speed control.

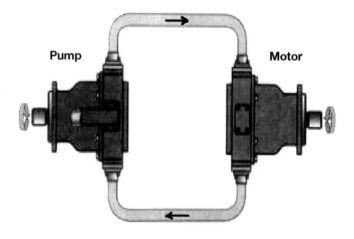

Pump   Motor

This is a closed-center hydraulic circuit in the most basic simplified form. Vickers Mobile Hydraulics Manual

HYDRAULIC REMOTES

Outlets and connectors for remote hydraulics are available on many of the larger garden and compact tractors. These provide pressurized oil to operate hydraulic cylinders or motors. Single-acting cylinders can only extend under pressure, and need gravity or springs to close or retract. Double-acting

Front ballast with suitcase weights is used on a Kubota L4400 FWA tractor to balance weight of 3PL slasher on back. Kubota

cylinders are pressurized by the valve in either direction, extension, or retraction. The retracting stroke is faster, but it has less thrust.

HYDRAULIC COUPLERS

Hydraulic couplers have been universally standardized to permit the ready connection and transfer of the fluid power to the remote actuators. Two systems, open-center or closed-center hydraulic circuit designs, are used on compact tractors. With open-center systems, any pump flow not directed by the directional control valve flows freely to the hydraulic reservoir. The problem is that it generates waste heat. With a fixed-displacement pump in a closed-center system, a smaller pump charges an accumulator, which together with the pump provides the flow on demand and heat loss is reduced.

Electric linear actuators are an alternative system for achieving powered linear movement without the need for hydraulics at a remote location around the tractor or implement. These use the tractor's electrics to energize a motor geared down to turn a screw jack for linear motion. An application on a garden tractor is the mower deck power lift.

John Deere's HX15 trailed shaft-driven, triple-gang, wing-fold rotary mower cuts 15 feet and requires a minimum of 55 horsepower. Deere's Flex-Wing ground suspension system minimizes bouncing by a combination of air springs with shock absorbers on wheel brackets. John Deere

CHAPTER 5
MOWING TRACTORS AND TRACTOR MOWERS

The difference between mowing tractors and tractor mowers is that mowing tractors are ride-ons and self-propelled mowing machines. Tractor mowers are mowers used with tractors or whatever else might pull or carry them. Bear in mind the distinction between consumer versus commercial mowers. Consumer units are lighter, cheaper, and designed for low hours of use versus heavier-duty, more durable commercial mowers. The United States has a healthy range of mower choices with over 40 brands of mowers, and 33 different zero turn mowers.

WHY MOW?

Turf grasses are abused more than practically any other vegetation. Repeatedly trodden down, macheted, crushed, and deluged; as soon as they stick their heads up, a mower comes along and cuts them down to size again. Yet they are expected to still look green and sharp. The goal of mowing, and all that goes with it, is grass management. Grass surfaces are mowed to either encourage leaf growth or to control unwanted or excessive vegetation. The more that healthy grass is mowed, the thicker it becomes. The thicker the grass is, the more traffic a lawn or turf can bear. A healthy green lawn is a pleasure to look at, enjoy, and use, as long as the amount of maintenance is reasonable. On the other hand, regular cutting restricts root development by continually forcing

Dixon Grizzly is a side-discharge triple disc. Dixon

Shown here is a three-point rear-mount, Deere MX6 mower on a model 4610 tractor. John Deere

plants to regrow foliage rather than putting energies into root growth. Playing fields with shallow roots are more vulnerable to foot traffic that can be caused by a cleated player's shoes or overuse. Grass repeatedly cut close to the ground needs very careful management because its reserves are low. Surface treatments, water management, and aerification are accordingly critical to root growth and greens care.

CONTROLLING WEEDS AND VEGETATIVE GROWTH

Different types of cutting equipment is needed depending on the vegetation, ranging from finishing mowers to sickle bars, heavy-duty slashers, mulchers, and brush or bush hogs. Mowing jobs and their equipment can be categorized as follows:

Rough-cut scrub, weeds, or uneven terrain with stones and other obstacles. For this type of work, a slasher, flail-type chopper, or other type of heavy-duty rotary mower with swinging blades that can handle obstacles would be selected.

Heavy-growth pasture that is free of stones but has gopher mounds, anthills, or levees could call for a rotary multidisc-type mower.

Pastures or verges that do not need to be cut too close to the ground can be maintained with a sickle bar, disc, or rotary mower. These are sometimes called rough-cut mowers. As far as rotary mowers are concerned, machines with multiple disc blades leave a neater, more uniform finish, and follow contours better than large single-spindle rotary mowers, depending on their mounting style. They can also be operated to leave a swath that is more readily collected or baled later.

Trimming fairways or big lawns where a good finish is desired. Scalping is of concern here. These mowers use multiblade rotary, gangs of single-spindle units, or reel-type mowers. They may also be called finishing or grooming mowers.

Fine-cut and very close trim greens are essential on golf courses, grass tennis courts, bowling greens, and some sports arenas. These surfaces need well-maintained and carefully sharpened reel-type mowers. In skilled hands, the height can be set to cut as low as ⅒th inch (2.5mm) and gauged to the nearest millimeter.

The home backyard lawn options are ride-ons, walk-behind self-propelled mowers, and robotic mowers. These machines are commonly of the single vertical-spindle rotary type or reel type.

Portable cutting machines include yard trimmers, brush cutters, and weed eaters with metal, plastic, or fiber cutterheads, but are not covered in this book.

GRASS CUTTING FUNDAMENTALS

Plant cutting takes place when blades sever the material. That can be done by high-speed impact, by sawing, by biting, or by lower-speed counter-edge shearing. In every case, sharp edges are needed for clean and efficient cutting. There are a lot of machine options with as many as 40 mower manufacturers, many machine models, and very different cutting conditions.

Basic information needed in choosing a plant-cutting machine, such as what has to be cut, how large of an area, what time to do the job, and what manpower and machine resources are available. Probably the most immediate question for grounds managers or contractors contemplating a mowing machine purchase has to do with economics and involves figuring out which machine is the most cost-effective. For example, how do the annual costs of mowing with a certain unit compare with a rental or leasehold? Would it

be more economical to acquire a wide-area mower (WAM) with a 12-foot cut, or two zero turns cutting 6 foot each, but requiring two operators?

CUTTING EDGES

The amount of energy and power needed to cut grass depends greatly on how sharp the mowing blades are and whether there is recutting. Dull or bent blades leave ragged leaf edges that bleed plant reserves and can be prone to invasion by harmful organisms. There is an art to blade sharpening to provide the best edge and correct angle. Resharpening blades on rotaries is fairly straightforward, but specialist equipment is essential for sharpening reel mowers and their bed knives. Replacement blades match the cutting deck for length, shape, and method of attachment.

MULCHING MOWERS

As long as the grass isn't too long, mulching benefits lawns. Since the clippings may be up to 85 percent water, they will quickly break down and recycle nutrients. Several approaches are used to encourage simultaneous mulching and mowing. Mulching blades may be suitably shaped to lift and carry material. Blade tilt adds lift to bring clippings up to where they have a chance to be cut several times and are better conveyed. Recutters can be double blades or circumferential screens close to the periphery of the rotary cutter. Mulching decks take a little more power.

COLLECTING CLIPPINGS

Cutterheads create lift and draft assist to deliver clippings to where they are collected or discharged. Decks may come with side discharge or center delivery. Collection and removal of clippings is mostly done for cosmetic reasons, unless lawn growth is heavy and has gotten ahead of schedule. Side discharge is the simplest for mowers. If the job calls for a big catcher, an additional impeller can be side mounted to drive the clippings back into the rear-mounted catcher. Big jobs and multiple-head decks may call for center discharge where a separate impeller is used to drive the clippings into the onboard container. Hydraulic high-lift mechanisms enable the container to be dumped over the side of trucks or into trailers.

RIDE-ON MOWERS
Mounting the Mower Deck
Mower attachments may be trailed and PTO- or engine-driven, or they can be semi- or fully mounted on the tractor by a hinge system, parallel linkage, or 3PL. Choice of mowing deck size is determined by the area to be covered,

A midmount riding mower by JCB Sales Limited.

frequency of mowing, crop to be cut, and, to some extent, desired stubble height.

Configuration

The position of the mower deck governs the machine configuration, and thus the engine and/or operator position. Decks that are fully mounted on the machine chassis for transport (although not necessarily while cutting, as on zero-turn mowers) can be rear-, mid-, or front-mounted and may have wing units to the side(s) as well. Swing-away/outrigger cutters are available that enable cutting close around posts. Engine position may also be behind, under, or in front of the operator. One advantage for a rear engine arrangement is that it opens up the view to the front and puts engine noise and exhaust behind the operator.

ZERO-TURN MOWERS

Zero turn mowers use castoring wheels on the front axle for support and balance. Zero turns steer by braking the inside drive wheel and powering the outer wheel, or by hydrostats with one driving wheel forward and the other in neutral (or in reverse for spot turns). Zero turns are popular with contractors, golf courses, and commercial work in areas that require the highest degree of maneuverability and involve trim work. Because zero turns can be shorter in overall length than conventional ride-ons, they take up less trailer space and are superior in tight areas. Their low center of gravity improves stability on hillsides. The deck size ranges from 48 to 72 inches and comes in stamped/pressed steel, fabricated steel, or cast alloy. Durability of the deck depends largely on the thickness of the steel.

The 33 models of zero turns on the market fall into two main categories: front- or mid-mount mower decks. The front-mount zero turns has the mower deck completely in front of the machine's body. This design is superior for poking under trees, re-entrant corners, and trimming

around tree rings and shrubs, etc. The drive wheels are under the operator with front-axle castering behind the deck. The deck is more accessible and can be flipped up to work on the mower in some models. The mid-mount zero turns has the drive wheels and caster wheels wrapped around the mower deck. Mid-mounts are less flexible for trimming, but are still highly maneuverable. Consider the serviceability of the deck when buying a zero turns mower. Service time will be less with a flip-up because the deck is capable of being rotated up to 90 degrees for blade access. A flip-up deck also saves trailer space.

WIDE-AREA MOWERS

Many compact tractor components have been incorporated into the design of wide-area mowers (WAM). These are finishing mowers designed for high productivity on fairways and for larger areas over 50 acres. For example the Jacobsen HR-9016 with 16-foot triple deck can mow 16 ½ acres an hour at an average 6 miles per hour and could easily cover 50 acres in a day, even with a lot of turns and maneuvering around obstacles. The WAMs have to include trailed units, as well as the self-propelleds. They come with 3 to 11 gangs for contour-following capability and wing-fold for transport.

CUTTERHEAD TYPES

Reel or Cylinder Mowers

Imagine cutting a golf green to precisely one-tenth of an inch height for the U.S. Open golf championship. Only a reel or cylinder mower can do that! Reel mowers, the original mowers, are designed for the finest turf finish until laser mowers become commercially available. Critical components of the reel mower are the front roller that governs cutting height, the reel itself with its spiraled cutting blades, and the bed knife which is the fixed counter-edge for the scissor action. A rear roller is used to stabilize and leave behind an attractive striping effect after each pass. Support wheels are often used for transport or to drive the reel. Hydraulic motor-driven reel mowers for the finest turf work have 10 to 12 blade reels and up to four cuts per inch

Dixon's Kodiak ZTR is a midmount zero-turn mower with a 50-inch deck. Dixon

of travel. The intermediate quality cutting comes from reels of 8-inch diameter with 5 or 6 blades that provide two cuts per inch of forward travel. The quality of cutting is governed by the number of blades, diameter and rotational speed of the reel, and machine forward speed. Blade sharpening and blade-to-bed clearance are critical. Specialized machines are available for sharpening both the bed knife and the reel blades. Mower reels are fairly durable and may require sharpening once a season. The bed knife needs frequent sharpening—even daily for tending top quality greens—and usually needs replacing more than once each season. For the fairways and larger areas, reel mowers are pulled behind the tractor in gangs. The power required is around 2.5 horsepower per foot of cut.

Concern for oil spills or leaks on golf greens has triggered a solution from John Deere's turf care division in Raleigh, North Carolina. Three 48-volt brushless electric motors power the three individual reels instead of hydraulics. The 2500E Hybrid Tri-Plex Greens Mower, released in 2005, eliminates 102 potential hydraulic leak points. The variable-speed electric motors are also reversible for cylinder sharpening and maintenance.

Rotary Mowers

Both single-vertical and multidisc-vertical axle types are available in rotary mowers. The single axle types used with compact tractors come in blade widths from 1½ to 6 feet. The great advantage of rotary cutters is their simplicity and ruggedness. The drawbacks are that they are noisy and dangerous. Their 200-mile-per-hour blades can instantly sever body parts that get in harm's way. They also throw objects great distances, so operators of rotary mowers should use all reasonable shields or guards and ensure that there are no bystanders within 300 feet.

Rotary mowers are categorized into three classes. Finishing or grooming mowers have multiple small wheels or rollers for more precise cutting height control and to minimize scalping a lawn. Ride-ons typically use a mid- or front-mount mower-deck configuration that makes it more comfortable for the operator to see what the cutter is doing. Front-mounts are highly maneuverable and advantageous for reaching under trees and into re-entrant corners, especially when fitted to a zero-turn chassis. Some designs use more than one cutting head designed to throw the clippings to the side or rear into containers for collection and removal from the lawn area.

Jacobsen's Fairway model 405 reel mower has seven 26-inch-wide reels that cut a 13.2-foot swath with a 46.5-horsepower diesel engine and 4WD. The reel units are available in either 7- or 11-knife heads depending on degree of fineness of cut required on the greens. Jacobsen

This is Deere's electric reel drive on the Triplex Greens Mower. John Deere

Disc or multidisc mowers use a series of turtles or smaller discs 18 to 22 inches in diameter that revolve at speeds up to 3,000 rpm and carry two or three blades that are arranged side by side. The turtles are timing gear driven so the blades overlap to avoid streaking. They are designed to cut close to the ground and are used to cut tall grasses or hay that will dry and be baled. They are available in sizes up to 9 feet for compact tractors.

Rough-cut rotaries are designed for heavy cutting and rough work and are not intended to be used close to the ground. They can chew up brush and mangle light saplings up to 2 inches in diameter with their heavy, swiveling blades. Cutting height is controlled by gauge wheel(s). They

Kesmac trailed nine-gang, reel-type fairway mower. Kesmac

are most often rear mounted or trailed, which makes for a long outfit that is not so readily maneuverable. They are made in 3 1/2- to 7-foot-wide decks for compact tractors.

ADJUSTING ROTARIES FOR BEST CUTTING

A useful rule about mowing lawns is not to cut too low. It is best to cut only the top third of the grass blades to promote thicker, healthier growth. Cutting too low can damage the root system, create a thatch problem, or scalp the turf. The problem is exacerbated the wider the deck. Single-disc rotary mowers that are not finishing mowers should not be used closer than about 3 inches. Finally, don't mow too fast. Choose a speed that gives an even cut.

MOWER DECK SUSPENSION

Mower deck suspension affects the way the deck and cutting heights are adjusted. Ground-following decks are used on most compact tractors. Linkages lift the mower deck for transport and pull the deck along while mowing;

but do not carry the weight of the deck when in use. That way the mower will follow the contours of the ground, independent of the tractor. Gauge wheels, usually pneumatic tires, or rollers govern deck height. In the transport position with ground-following decks, the deck is raised fully by linkage. Cutting height gauge wheels should be adjusted using the alignment holes or collar bushings with the machine on a level surface and the engine switched off. Suspended decks are found on most smaller mowers, garden tractors, and some compact mowing tractors. Suspended decks hang under the machine on a parallelogram linkage and do not rely on gauge wheels. Skids, wheels, or rollers are there only to prevent scalping on uneven ground. A calibrated knob or lever-controlled adjustable stop limits linkage movement and determines deck height. The deck is lowered until the linkage hits the stop and the deck is suspended there.

Belly-mount mowers are a bit more tricky than others to adjust, but the time spent setting up a mid-mount

65

Kubota M105 with 3PL Gehl disc mower. Kubota

mower on a flat surface is repaid in the quality of finish and extending the life of the blades.

Three-point linkage–mounted mower adjustments should be operated with the tractor sway bars reasonably tight, which is especially critical if you back up with the mower running. It should be free to pivot vertically—within limits—about the lower link balls so the mower can flex over bumps and hollows. In operation, all rotary mowers should be set up with the front slightly lower than the rear of the deck (say 1/4 inch on smaller decks and 1/2 inch on a 5-foot mower) to minimize recutting and reduce power demand. The deck also needs to be level from side to side.

Setup needs to be done on a flat, level surface. A few minutes spent properly setting up the deck will enhance the mower's performance in terms of cut and power consumption.

DISCHARGING CLIPPINGS

Rotaries are excellent for mulching clippings, and some designs have mulching devices to specifically enhance that feature. The aim is either to spread the clippings evenly back onto the mown surface or discharge the clippings into a container or swath for later collection. Mower decks are designed for side or rear discharge.

A DMD disc mower parked on its stand. Note the series of turtles or individual disc cutters. The 5½-foot 3PL model requires the power of a 35-horsepower tractor. Buy Smart Inc.

This swivel-hitch tongue is designed for great turning capability, cutting over square corners, and narrow headlands. New Hollands's 9.1-foot discbine mower-conditioner with its seven discs requires a 65-horsepower tractor. CNH

Kubota's GR riding mower with suspended deck. Kubota

Rotaries take some power since blade top speeds can be in the 200-mile-per-hour range. The power is typically 2 horsepower per foot of cut for light-duty rotary mowing and 5 horsepower per foot of cut for brush hogs capable of smashing 2-inch-diameter saplings.

ENGINE-FUNCTIONED OR SELF-POWERED MOWER UNITS

One way to greatly increase cutting width and boost mowing capacity is to tow an engine-powered mower along the side of the tractor-mower. Trailed, separate-engine-functioned mowers are available for towing behind the smallest tractors, utility vehicles, or ATVs. Usually, a set of four wheels govern the cutting height. A 5-foot heavy-duty trailed unit, for example, may have up to a 15-horsepower engine on board.

FLAIL MOWERS

The horizontal-axle flail-type mower appeals to highway maintenance and park managers because flail mowers don't throw objects to the side or as far as other mowers. The free-swinging blades cut by impact. The grass finish is not as

Time spent setting the 3PL system for the best cut will be repaid in terms of better finish, less recutting, and a longer life of the mower blades. A Kubota M95S is shown here. Kubota

even as for a vertical-shaft mower. The power is typically 4 horsepower per foot of cut.

Boom mowers use a flail cutterhead on a highly maneuverable, hydraulically controlled arm. These can be used to cut brush and weeds in areas where other types of mowers are impractical, such as steep slopes, ditches and verges, woody hedgerows, and over fences or posts.

Sickle bars are in a class of their own. They use fixed guards and a set of sharp blades mounted in a reciprocating knife-back that passes through the guards. Sickle bar

mowers for tractors are side mounted. They don't recut the vegetation, take little power, and are excellent for cutting tall growth without plugging. The reciprocating blades of a sickle bar (or the two counteracting sickles in the case of a balanced sickle bar) are vulnerable if they meet an obstruction, such as a fence post. A break-back arrangement on the bar allows them to swing back, but then they have to be reset. Knife section wear can be rapid and that means high maintenance. Because they use less power and are lighter, sickle bars can be wider—up to 10 feet for the same power

John Deere's all-wheel-steer LX277 ride-on mowing tractor with side-discharge mower deck. John Deere

input as a 3-foot rotary. The knife sections are usually at a 3-inch pitch and run at up to 1,800 strokes per minute for balanced cutterbars. Knife sections may need attention several times in a season. Power is typically 0.5 horsepower per foot of cut.

SLOPE-MOWING TRACTORS

Slope mowers are purpose-built machines for steep slope operation, and some are even suited to 45 degrees or 100 percent slope! Regular ride-ons generally become hazardous over 20 percent (110) slope, but they can be hazardous if mishandled on even shallower inclines. It should probably come as no surprise that some innovative compact tractor designs for working on slopes come from mountainous Switzerland. For example, Aebi & Co. AG of Burgdorf, Switzerland, offers their Terratrac series for grounds maintenance and challenging terrain. Typical of sidehill tractors, the low center of gravity and the wide wheelbase give safer slope-handling capability. Nevertheless, tipping is an ever-present hazard, so a four-post ROPS-integrated safety frame, along with an operator-constraining seat belt, are essential for slope work and are highly desirable elsewhere.

STAND-ON MOWERS

Stand-on mowers have a valuable niche in the mower market—their popularity climbed when operators found that the stand-on mode of operation had several advantages

This is a trailed three-gang rotary finishing mower for golf course fairways. Woods' 17-foot model requires a minimum 40-horsepower tractor. Woods Equipment

compared with riding. The overall machine is also shorter and takes up less room on transport vehicles. A stand-on mower has bail-out ability (BOA) in the event of danger. If the operator gets into trouble on a steep slope, he steps off and the engine immediately shuts down.

By contrast, the seat, armrests, and control levers confine the operator on a ride-on, which makes it

Shown here is a Befco trailed mower with its own engine; in this case, mounted on its own wheels. A utility vehicle may tow it. A 10.5-horsepower Briggs & Stratton engine drives a 5-foot three-bladed rotary mower. Befco

A Swisher front-mount mower with its own engine that adapts readily to use with an ATV or UV. Swisher Inc.

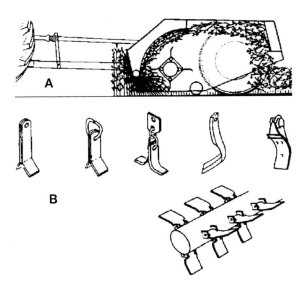

This is an illustration of a flail mower plus the range of cutter blades for the horizontal-shaft cutterhead. CGIR /ASAE Handbook of Agricultural Engineering

Bomford's boom-mounted flail mower is shown here with its own hydrostatic power pack on the back of the tractor. A wrist mount of the hydraulic motor-driven cutterhead means it can be used to trim hedges, as well as reach over fences or posts along a roadside. Bomford-Turner Ltd.

The Befco sicklebar mower is a balanced design with sickle and guards oscillating counter to each other. Befco

This is an example of the DewEze rear-discharge slope mowers by Harper Industries Inc. Model ATM 72LC, the All-Terrain Machine, has a 30-horsepower engine, two-part 72-inch deck, and self-leveling chassis. There are hydraulic drives throughout and the body remains level while the cutting head follows contours and is capable of slopes to 66 percent or 34 degrees. DewEze

DANGER
Deflector or entire grass
catcher must be in place
before mowing

DANGER
KEEP HANDS and FEET AWAY

A mulching attachment for the
Dixon Kodiak ZTR is shown here.
Dixon

25°

Wright Manufacturing's Sentar has
been a pioneer in stand-on mower
development. An operator can also shift
from standing to sitting and back again
while mowing. The operator can adjust
the mower's weight distribution on the
fly in response to problem situations or
to increase traction and can quickly
dismount. It has self-neutralizing
control handles. The 61-inch-deck
model has a 23-horsepower Kohler
engine as one of the engine options.

Shown here is an AgriMetal greens aerator/vertical mulcher. AgriMetal

Toro's ProCore 648 greens aerator
pulls cores as deep as 4 inches over
a 48-inch-wide swath. The
operator-controlled tractor has
three-wheel drive. Toro

Grasshopper's AERA-Vator doesn't pull plugs, but the tines penetrate the turf vertically and agitate to fracture hard soil and create more pore space with minimal surface disruption. Turf can be overseeded or ground can be topdressed immediately following treatment, and there are no cores to clean up prior to pedestrian or sports field use. The AERA-Vator uses timed, vibrating tines to fracture the soil and relieve compaction in 40- and 60-inch sizes. Grasshopper

difficult to exit in an emergency. Not only that, but a stand-on can handle slope mowing better because the operator standing on the very low platform becomes an active part of the machine's weight distribution. A stationary gripping bar above the dashboard provides fingertip controls.

LAWN HEALTH EQUIPMENT: DETHATCH-ERS, HARROWS, AERATORS, AND APPLICATORS

Over time, turf and lawns become tight, compacted from traffic and root-bound, or accumulate too much thatch and clippings. In any case, healthy growth is impeded. Thatch is a layer of dead and living shoots, stems, and leaf clippings that accumulate below the green tops. Thatch accumulates faster as cutting height increases. When thatch decomposes and becomes intermingled with soil particles it is called

mat. A small amount of mat and thatch is beneficial, but when thatch exceeds $\frac{1}{4}$ to $\frac{3}{8}$ inch thick, it retards quality turf growth. Dethatchers use spring tines to loosen and rake up the thatch that can be subsequently collected and moved. Turf slicers and aerators cut turf-grass rhizomes, tillers, and thatch. Some designs punch through thatch to perforate the surface, lift out soil cores, or do both. Compact, tractor-mounted scarifiers and aerators may need extra weight for penetration. Top-dressers should follow aeration to spread porous material to fill the core holes and prevent them from closing in. Spring tooth arrows may be used to spread the top-dressing sand and further disperse thatch and soil cores. Leaf rakes, broom sweepers, and collectors are useful for tidying up a green area. Each of these tools readily mounts on the three-point or other hitches of mowing tractors, often using hydraulic motor drives.

CHAPTER 6
THE WIDER PERSPECTIVE: COMPACT SELF-PROPELLED MOBILE MACHINES

THE GREEN INDUSTRY

Finding and keeping suitable labor is probably one of the greatest problems that many industries face. Reliable labor is hard to find, and labor is often the highest expense item in an enterprise. Compact equipment comes into its own to get jobs done fast with less labor. Compact tractor variants and self-propelling (SP) machines used by groundskeepers, landscape contractors, golf course managers, turf farms, and small-scale farms might be labeled the green industry, which is said to be the fastest-growing segment of agriculture. The number of acres under turf or managed grassland, such as roadside verges, is creeping up on the size of the

Above and oveleaf: Kubota's L39 TLB is shown in action. Support stands for stability on backhoe work are hydraulically retractable and lowering the bucket with the double-acting bucket tilt cylinders lifts the front axle for extra stability. Kubota

Kubota

country's wheat acreage. While compact tractors, garden tractors, ride-on mowers, and tractors equipped with mowers may be the most visible use for compact tractors, the range certainly doesn't end there. All the compact machines used by contractors, the construction industry, and rental-service yards use tractor technologies and are in high demand to reduce labor costs. Some of the machines included are tractor-loader backhoes, skid-steer or tracked loaders, mini-loaders, mini-earthmovers, and work utility vehicles.

COMPACT CONSTRUCTION, CONTRACTOR, AND GREENS EQUIPMENT
INTEGRATED TRACTOR-LOADER-BACKHOES (TLBS)

Compact industrial TLBs come equipped with or require higher flow-rate hydraulics than compact tractors usually put out. Current designs use two-lever/four-way joystick controls (earlier versions had four-lever controls) that manage the swing, inner boom, outer boom, and bucket curl functions. The stabilizer hydraulics use separate controls.

Deere's 33-PTO-horsepower model 110 purpose-built TLB shows the two operating positions and the degree of working visibility with the two backhoe positions superimposed. The backhoe arm can carry other attachments. John Deere

Integrated backhoes are rigidly mounted onto the tractor chassis. Add-on backhoes are usually lighter built with restricted digging depth of 6 to 10 feet, compared to 14 feet for heavier-duty dedicated TLBs. A backhoe is one of the most expensive attachments for compacts. Mounting and operating a backhoe takes skill and experience. Experience and extra care are needed to avoid tipping a TLB or hitting objects or people in the swing mode. There are a couple of light-duty backhoe alternatives—three-point hitch-mounted units and trailed units. Trailed backhoes usually come with

their own engine and hydraulic pack. Backhoe buckets are made in a range of sizes matched to machine power. They include standard, trenching, and thumb buckets, along with ripper and claw attachments.

SKID-STEER OR TRACKED LOADERS

High maneuverability, tight turns, and versatility characterize this class of tractors with engines and unit sizes that range from 30 to 120 horsepower. Bobcat licensed the original Keller design and the Bobcat Company now offers a wide

JCB's FEL/backhoe model 2CX. JCB Sales Limited

diversity of skid steers and attachments. For example, the Bobcat A220 has two steering modes: skid steer and all-wheel steer (AWS), as well as tracked models. Skid-steer mode turns on the spot for highest maneuverability, but this type of steering by its nature wears tires and can rough up soft ground. AWS mode is easier on tires at the expense of a wider turning radius, but leaves little surface disturbance.

OPERATIONAL ASPECTS OF SKID-STEER/TRACKED LOADER TRACTORS

The extreme maneuverability of skid-steer loaders is also a hazard; the operator is subject to violent action inside the capsule and the machine is not stable on rough country. For that reason, skid steers are equipped with total operator enclosure and seat restraints. All skid steers are required to have operator-constraining safety bars that prevent the machine from starting or its hydraulics from functioning unless the operator is on the seat. Most skid steers are used with loaders, so load lift capacity and lift height are key qualities. Loader arms are right next to the enclosure and obstruct vision in certain areas. The loader arms present a major hazard with several pinch points that require a cage on the enclosure to prevent the operator getting an arm caught in the lift mechanism. JCB's approach to that issue with their Robot models is to use a single arm on the right-hand side, which additionally allows side access to the operator's station. Boom locks are essential to prevent the loader from dropping on people when the operator is outside the machine while the arms are raised. Another aspect is that the higher the loader's groundspeed range, the better for fast cycling on jobs.

BUCKET LIFT MECHANISM

The smaller skid-steer models are usually capable of lifting to about 10 feet. In its simplest form, the lift arms describe a plain arc, which means the bucket moves rearward as it is lifted, and that is not convenient for unloading over the sideboards of a truck. To get around that, four-bar linkages are used on the latest machines. The linkage mechanism allows a parallel bucket lift that assists in reaching and dumping a load closer to the center of the truck bed. It is advantageous, but the added complexity of the boom mechanisms increases cost.

Hydrotransmissions permit instant directional changes. Inching capability provides the ability to apply high torque at very low speeds when approaching a load. Low-effort joystick controls are essential for the multiple control movements for such machines. The best designs have an ergonomic seat and armrests with controls laid out for an operator who spends a large part of the workweek inside the capsule. Visibility should be as unrestricted by boom arms as possible. Finally, ready hitch-up of equipment is important for fast exchange between attachment options. There are several choices of tires, including flat-proof solid tires that eliminate delays due to punctures. Where flotation and wheel rutting at the work site are problematic, tracked loader models or throw-on tracks that fit over the skid-steer wheels are available.

MINI-LOADERS

The stand-on compact utility loader, mini-loader, or mini-skid-steer concept originated in Australia around 1980 when a Queensland plumbing contractor built himself a 10-horsepower motorized wheelbarrow. From there a business developed. Demand grew rapidly Down Under, especially from equipment rental yards.

The Dingo was redesigned as a versatile hydraulic tool on wheels. After a partnership breakup, a competitive line emerged, the Kanga loader series. Not to be outdone, Dingo Mini-Diggers Pty. Ltd. lined up a contract with Toro in Minnesota to build Dingoes for the North and South American markets. Now the U.S. market has a dozen makers in the mini-skid loader business, including Toro, Ramrod (Kanga), ASV, Gravely, Finn, PowerTrac, Thomas, Bobcat, Gehl (Avant), Ditch Witch, Vermeer, and Multi-One.

Applications for these mini-loaders are ever growing; from landscaping and grounds maintenance, construction sites, internal demolition and high-rise construction, trenching, paving, snow removal, fencing contractors, cattle farms, foundries, and so on. Attachments are just as diverse: four-in-one buckets, vibrating plows, 30-inch tree-planting augers, trenchers, and rotor tillers. There are over 70 attachments available for these loaders, which are the equivalent of a Swiss Army Knife for contractors. Actually, many of these machines spend most of their time at anything but bucket work, such is the versatility of the hydraulically powered attachments.

The mini-skids are highly maneuverable machines, and some models are less than 32 inches wide and narrow enough to get through a garden gate or fit nicely on a regular car trailer. This ready transportability and versatility means they can do more work than six hand laborers. An important outlet for this type of machinery is the equipment rental business. Home Depot alone has 800 such outlets. Tracked models are useful where wheel tracks or flotation are problematic.

At the heart of the mini-skid is a complex of hydraulic pumps (up to four pumps on some models) that are stacked and directly connected to the engine and provide power to the ground and all the other attachments or outlets. The four pumps simultaneously direct hydraulic power to the traction system, loader functions, and auxiliary outlets for attachments.

Seating is an optional attachment on these machines, but stand-on operation has several advantages: simplicity and smaller overall machine size, excellent visibility, and the ability to rapidly get on and off.

In the United States, sales exceed 14,000 units a year and the mass marketers like Home Depot have entered the equipment rental business, some offering mini-loaders. Rental is a way around the price tag of a mini-loader, which are powered with engines from 10 to 28 horsepower and range in price from $10,000 to $28,000, not including attachments.

Small size and versatility are the key features of mini-skid loaders. They can be operated in walk-behind, stand-on, or seated mode. Not having a cab or all the operator comforts keeps costs down as well as facilitating operator access. The earliest models came from Australia, and with increasing sophistication, mini-skids are proliferating in North America where there are now a dozen brands offered with licensed or similar products. Some models have over 70 attachment options.

MINI-EXCAVATORS

I once had a garage foundation job and called up a local contractor to bring his skid steer with attachments. The task was tight for space near the house, so I was concerned there wouldn't be enough room to operate the machinery. When the morning came, the contractor showed up with a mini-excavator and quieted my concerns the moment he set to work. The machine was simply amazing! It did the job faster than a skid steer could have, with less site disturbance, and was quieter. When it comes to multiple jobs like digging trenches, leveling, breaking and lifting old concrete, drilling holes, or compacting in a restricted space with a time constraint, compact excavators are the

Bobcat's all-wheel-steer (AWS) loader. Model A300 with front-mount, laser controlled box scraper. Bobcat

way to go! These are arguably the most expensive piece of equipment in the compact tractor corral, but they are also the most versatile. Mini-excavators with engines in the 12- to 45-horsepower category are small enough to fit neatly into a trailer or light-to-medium tipper truck. A valuable attribute is that special permits are not needed to transport the machine between sites, unlike full-size excavators. Mini-excavators are made in two styles: tail swing (boom counterweighted and capable of working with a shorter track length) or zero tail swing (ZTS), which needs a longer track.

CHECKLIST
WHAT TO LOOK FOR IN A
MINI-LOADER

Outside dimensions, especially width, to match the type of work

Bucket type and size; loader lift capacity

Auxiliary hydraulic flow for attachments, such as augers or rotary hoes

Noise level and operator controls

Deere's ZTS series of compact excavators are part of the zero tail swing (ZTS) class of equipment. Here are some specifications:

	17 ZTS	27 ZTS	35 ZTS	50 ZTS
Engine Power (horsepower)	12.3	32	32	41.5
Operating Weight (tons)	1.9	3.3	3.9	5.1
Transport Length (feet)	12	13.9	15.4	17.4
Lift Capacity, over front at ground level and bucket extended 10 feet (pounds)	864	2,146	2,865	5,190
Max Digging Depth; Digging Reach (feet)	7.25; 12.9	8.7; 15.4	10.3; 17.1	11.8; 19

Cat's skid-steer model 236B. Catepillar Inc.

Above and overleaf: JCB builds the 190 Robot (70 net horsepower) tracked loader. This loader has several novel features, including a right-hand-side, low-slung loader arm that allows for side entry to the machine. Side entry is regarded as safer and more convenient for a skid steer. JCB Sales Limited

Some ingenious undercarriages that are options with the current breed of mini-excavators include models with telescoping tracks that enable the operator to narrow the machine to get past a tight area, then widen out again for stability at the job site; hydraulic tilt to maintain the digging body level on a slope and dig a straight vertical trench on uneven terrain to prevent underdigging, which can cause a trench to cave in; and side boom swing allows the excavator to pull in tight to a structure and still scoop without colliding with the structure.

Mini-excavators can be equipped with various buckets: combination, light material, tooth, and many other attachments, such as augers, rotary cutters, industrial grapples, and jackhammers. These machines can tackle all kinds of landscaping jobs—from grading and leveling to carrying concrete blocks and loading debris.

Vibratory compactors use a set of eccentric weights rotating inside the roller(s) to provide greater compaction compared to a plain roller.

UTILITY VEHICLES

ATVs will not be covered in this book because they are more often high-speed recreational types of vehicles. On the other hand, utility vehicles (UVs) are the fringe dwellers of the compact tractor field. These are machines that use tractor technology—similar engines, drivetrains, braking, function, and form—to produce all-terrain mini-trucks.

There probably isn't a golf course or greenskeeper without a corral full of these machines. For example, one 18-hole, 200-acre course in Ames, Iowa, has 51 UVs. Most of them are motorized golf carts, but more than a handful are deployed as work vehicles for the grounds staff who maintain the links and greens of 120 out of the 200 acres. The course manager likes the restricted speed of these service vehicles. The typical top speed is around 15 miles per hour, but that may be optional depending on transmission. Unskilled employees can't tear around and damage the links! These machines make the work flow smoothly by transporting people, hauling cargo, pulling equipment, picking up golf balls, and powering other special tools.

Since there are many engine and parts commonalities, a number of the compact tractor makers offer utility vehicles. Consider John Deere's Gator and ProGator lines, Toro's Workman, Cub Cadet's Big Country, Steiner Textron's Workhorse, and Polaris' Workmobile. These are often forward-control machines where the driver's seat is up front, ahead of the transmission, and in some cases is over the engine. This growing market can be divided into two

CHECKLIST
WHAT TO LOOK FOR IN A
MINI-EXCAVATOR

Zero tail swing or counterbalanced design

All-up weight—mini-excavators are first rated on total weight basis, e.g., 3-ton, 7-ton, 12-ton, etc.

The weight of the machine needs to be compatible with your existing transporting capabilities

Look at digging depth and reach; lift capacity; bucket type and size; backfill blade

Auxiliary hydraulic flow for attachments like augers or road breakers

Two-speed drive system and speeds

Fuel tank capacity

Noise level and operator comfort

CHECKLIST
WHAT TO LOOK FOR IN A
UTILITY VEHICLE

Tray size and capacity

Seating capacity for the number of people to be transported at any one time

Engine type and power

Transmission and speed limitations

Wheel configuration for traffic ability or floatation

Tray types and fitments—flatbeds, cargo beds, stake side, or van box

Tray lift—electric lift or hydraulic dump

Enclosed cab or ROPS frame

Consider operational aspects and speed limit if you are hiring unskilled drivers

The JCB 520 LoadAll. ASV Inc.

Bobcat's tracked Model T140 dumps truckside. Bobcat

classes: light- and heavy-duty utilities. The heavy-duty UV models can carry over 1 ton of cargo in the tray, which may be power tiltable. They are rugged, versatile, quiet, have a safe low profile, and are powered by up to 34-horsepower engines in either gasoline or diesel versions. The light-duty models, 10 to 16 horsepower, may carry up to half a ton payload in the tray. There are also intermediate models and 48-volt-battery, electric-powered versions. UVs have low-pressure tires for minimal turf surface marking and clutchless transmissions for driving simplicity. The E-Z-Go behaves like a golf cart—it starts and runs by releasing the brake and depressing the accelerator.

Bobcat uses liquid-cooled diesel engines on both its MT52 and MT55 Mini-Track Loaders. Despite their small size, they are said to do the work of 10 well-built laborers. Bobcat

Bobcat's MT52 is just 36 inches wide and the MT55 is 41.5 inches wide. If the operator moves away from the rear of the machine, the loader automatically stops. Bobcat

Toro Dingo's K9-3 hydraulic system is directly coupled to the 22-horsepower (16.4-kw) Kohler engine and has a 6 km/h top speed, bucket load capacity of 1,100 pounds, and an operating weight of 1,640 pounds. Toro

JCB has three Dumpster models with load capacities up to 2,000 pounds, including self-loading versions. JCB Sales Limited

A Kubota KX161 demonstrates the virtue of a ZTS design. Kubota

Kubota's KX71 is shown here with concrete-breaker attachment. A mini-excavator and a skid steer can replace a TLB for contract work. Kubota

93

A Kubota KX71 mini-excavator with side-swing boom is great for tight work near buildings and structures. Kubota

Bobcat's double-drum vibratory compactor. Bobcat

Deere's 6x4 Gator has a 1,000-pound-capacity tray. John Deere

Bobcat's Toolcat is arguably the most versatile of all UVs. Bobcat

Kubota's RTV900 general-purpose work vehicle is shown here in two different settings. Kubota

The Polaris Ranger is an example of the small utility vehicles built by ATV manufacturers. They can be purchased with four-wheel drive, and have solid off-road capability. When equipped with aftermarket tracks, as on the Mattracks-equipped Polaris on the opposite page, the Ranger becomes capable of crossing deep swamps and fresh snow. Lee Klancher

CHAPTER 7
COMPACT TRACTOR ATTACHMENTS— MATCHING TRACTOR TO THE JOB

MANY ATTACHMENTS

At first sight there's a bewildering choice of equipment that can be fitted to compact tractors. This chapter will run through a range and suggest the most suitable tractor and attachment combinations. At the end of each main section there will be a "What to look for" section. Mowers have been dealt with in Chapter 5, but many times other attachments can be fitted to a ride-on instead of the mower, which might even help balance the tractor. Selection will require knowing how big the jobs are, such as area covered, how frequently, and in what time frame. There is also the matter of cost. Usually there is a certain optimal size of attachment to do a job at the least cost. Determining the optimal point can't be done with precision unless you're in a business that has a lot of past data to be able to work it out. The graph (located on page 102) shows a size-optimization curve.

FRONT-END LOADERS FOR COMPACTS

Apart from mowers, the one tractor attachment that is more common than any other is the front-end loader (FEL). Many dealers sell up to 60 percent of their compact tractors with FELs. Uses include lifting, carrying, pushing, scraping, leveling, loading vehicles, lifting the front of the tractor for servicing (double-acting cylinders only), and pushing snow. There is a wide range of bucket types in addition to the common material bucket, such as four-in-one buckets with biting jaws or grapple capability and rock buckets. There are also loader attachments, including pallet forks, rock rakes, bale spears, push blades, and snowplows.

Tractor-loaders can be either integral with the tractor or attached and readily demounted. In some cases attaching/detaching the loader only takes minutes. If you are contemplating a lot of loader work, front-wheel assist and shuttle-shift or hydrostatic-drive transmissions for clutchless speedy changes from forward to reverse are desirable.

Counterweights should be installed on back of the tractor to balance the FEL-equipped tractor. There are two types of hydraulics on the simpler loaders: Single-acting hydraulic rams raise the arms and rely on gravity for lowering. Double-acting cylinders power both up and down, which is far more useful and speeds up cylinder retraction. Double-acting cylinders are essential on bucket tilt as well as more useful on loader arms for applying downward forces when digging, changing front tires, levering rocks, etc. As a safety note, the FEL should never be left alone with the loader arms raised. It is both hazardous and a strain on the hydraulics, especially if the machine is left out in the midday sun.

BLADES

Front blades are far easier to use than rear blades and come as either FEL attachments or with their own hydraulics and arms. Rear blades are available with 180-degree swing and options include angling and tilting capability. The same loader arms can be used with rotary brooms that may be PTO- or ground-driven. Rotary brooms are usually angled, which makes them handy for cleaning hard surfaces, such as driveways or roads, and clearing light snow. Rear 3PL blades are a cheaper option but they have the disadvantage of craning the neck during use. Blades and brooms obviously leave the best finish when they are wider than the tractor. Sweeper-collectors can be mounted on loader arms and have a float feature to follow ground contours independently of the tractor.

FRONT THREE-POINT LINKAGE (3PL)

Front 3PLs are an aftermarket accessory in North America, but deploying a front linkage in Europe is commonplace to carry out several functions with narrower equipment in one field pass. The front linkage can come factory installed on some brands, such as Fastrac.

Box scrapers and scoops can do many things beyond what a loader can do around building and landscaping sites. They also might be considered a cheaper and less capable alternative to an FEL for shifting dirt laterally. These useful 3PL attachments can be used to push, pull, or carry soil; and box scrapers are often sold with adjustable ripper teeth on the front toolbar for loosening the ground.

CarryAlls are very handy for reforestation. The CarryAll is a 3PL-mounted platform that mounts on the front or rear linkage or even on loader arms. Pallet forks, trays, and boxes on loader arms or 3PL are ideal for compact tractors used for vegetable production. The forks may be the fixed or floating-tine types.

TILLAGE EQUIPMENT

All kinds of tillage implements, from harrows to subsoilers, are available for compact tractors. The size of the implements depends on soil type and tilling depth, ranging from implements that would be somewhat wider than the tractor down to single-shank rippers that will stall a compact trying to work at 12 inches depth. Rigid shank tools are suitable only for rock- and stump-free land. Where you have those obstructions, use spring-trip or shear-bolt protected tools to preserve both the implement and tractor.

Cultivators are available in rigid or spring shank, narrow or sweep tine, and toolbar or floating-gang style. Rotary tillers have the advantage of once-over cultivation, and they can convert short vegetated areas into a seedbed in one pass. A hinged flap on the back controls the degree of clod shatter. There are two types of rotary tillers that rotate the blades in the same direction as the tractor wheels and are easy to pull. They can even push the tractor. The more aggressive reverse-rotation type of rotary hoe or rotavator is useful for breaking up hard soils. Rotary cultivators call for 7 to 15 horsepower per foot worked, depending on the depth of cultivation.

TRENCHERS

Three-point linkage–trencher diggers and augers are often part of a contractor's kit as attachments for mini-loaders.

HAYING EQUIPMENT FOR COMPACT TRACTORS

Today hay balers are available in very different sizes. Compact tractors up to 25 horsepower can power mini-roll and small square balers which make bales 3 feet wide by 2 feet diameter for the mini-roll (45 pound bales) and 13x18-inch cross-section by 4¼ feet long (up to 60-pound bales) for the mini-square. Bale weights depend on hay moisture and crop variety. Heavier-duty, small square balers that can pack

BUCKETS AND ATTACHMENTS AVAILABLE FOR FRONT-END LOADERS

Light/Standard/Heavy-Duty Buckets
Four-in-One Bucket
Grapple
Pallet Forks/Lifter
Bale Spear
Crane Hook
Blade: Straight/Tilting/Angle
Rock Bucket
Sweeper
Front Blade
Carryall

a 100-pound bale take more power, such as 50 horsepower. A matching sickle bar mower, tedder, and/or side-delivery rake will be needed to round out the small hay bale business. For top quality hay, a mower-conditioner is desirable for more uniform drying between stems and leaves in a crop like alfalfa and to minimize leaf loss. The highest feed nutrition is in the leaves.

ATTACHMENTS FOR WORKING WITH TREES

A tree spade is an ingenious mechanism for preparing holes, lifting out an established tree, and placing it into a prepared hole. Vermeer has several models of tree spades in trailed-, tractor-, or truck-mounted versions; and Bobcat has a unit that mounts on the skid steer's loader arms.

Log splitters are designed to prepare firewood. They come in vertical and horizontal types with the vertical splitter for heavier logs. Tractor-powered splitters usually need two people to operate, one to handle the log and one at the control handle. For safety, the tractor hydraulics must be

The following table gives some notional front-end loader (FEL) sizes for a given tractor power range.

Tractor PTO Power	FEL Bucket Width (feet); Breakout (pounds)
10 to 2 5	4; 950
25 to 40	5; 1,800
40 to 55	7; 3,500
55 to 75	7; >3,500

Machinery matching—the size of machine attachment for the least operating cost for example—can be determined if there is a database of past machinery usage to work with. Otherwise, general guidelines will have to suffice. You won't find answers in a textbook because there are so many variables in each application. In this example for a 3PL-mounted mower on a 50-horsepower tractor, the 6-foot model would be the most economical.

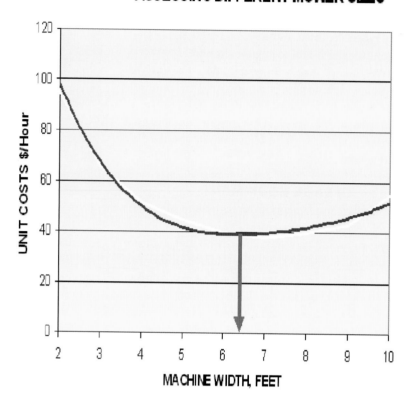

O&O COSTS 50 HP TRACTOR / MOWER - ASSESSING DIFFERENT MOWER SIZES

(vertical axis: UNIT COSTS $/Hour; horizontal axis: MACHINE WIDTH, FEET)

CHECKLIST
WHAT TO LOOK FOR IN A
FRONT END LOADER

Integral with tractor or quick attach

Loader arms to match the type of work

Rugged construction

Range of bucket types; load arms' lift capacity

Parallel bucket lift

Height of dump

Ease of swapping bucket or other attachment

Convenience of operator controls

Shuttle shift transmission

connected to a separate valve block on the splitter to prevent the person maneuvering the log from being caught by the splitter.

STUMP GRINDERS

Tractor PTO-driven, 3PL stump grinders use a power wheel tipped with tungsten carbide teeth to chew away at tree stumps. In the landscaping business the stump is often ground down below the soil surface and the hole is back-filled. Tractor-mounted models are not as agile as independent self-powered grinders. During use, the operator must remain vigilant to keep away bystanders, avoid thrown objects, and to always stop the machine when approaching the grinder.

POSTHOLE DIGGERS AND POST DRIVERS

Compacts are often used for fencing with PTO-driven, 3PL posthole diggers and/or post drivers. Earth augers also relieve the tedious job of planting holes for trees. Tractor-powered augers have caused many accidents. They should not be operated alone or by persons wearing loose clothing.

SPREADERS

Distributing fertilizers and chemical ameliorants with 3PL and trailed spreaders is a common practice with compact tractors. Granular droppers, spinner, and pendulum spreaders dominate. Application uniformity is key to effective spreading so you need to calibrate it in accord with the product label.

Kubota BX2230 with FEL and midmount mower with grass collector. Kubota

A Kubota TLB-equipped Model L39 is dumping over truckside. Kubota

SPRAYERS

Many types of chemicals are applied in farming, from plant nutrients to herbicides to pesticides to fumigants, and they come in all forms, including granules, powders, gases, and liquids. Insecticide and herbicide applicators for compact equipment range from spray booms to weed wipers. Boom spraying is one way to cover an area rapidly. Three-point linkage–mounted spray rigs use a PTO-driven pump to pressurize the boom or spray wands. There are two categories of weed-control chemicals: contact and systemic. Spraying is notoriously inefficient at targeting pests so care is needed in handling noxious compounds. Dress appropriately for the job and wear a respirator, goggles, gloves, boots, long sleeves and pants, and sometimes a chemical-resistant suit, and minimize spray drift. Skills are also necessary to get the best out of the chemical and calibrate the sprayer. Spray drift into nontarget areas is a serious problem. Good application involves a uniform, accurate application at the prescribed rate. Spray nozzle choice is a tradeoff between spraying fine droplets to get maximum coverage versus spray drift which worsens as the droplets get finer. Spray boom height is critical in managing application uniformity and

This is an aftermarket front 3PL made by LaForge for Deere's larger tractors.
H. Defranq. LaForge France

Kubota FEL and box scraper are shown here on a model L4400. Kubota

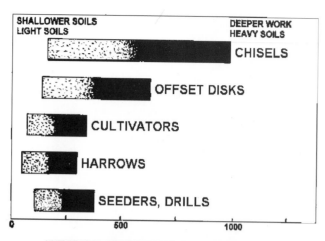

SHALLOWER SOILS
LIGHT SOILS   DEEPER WORK
HEAVY SOILS

CHISELS

OFFSET DISKS

CULTIVATORS

HARROWS

SEEDERS, DRILLS

0   500   1000

UNIT DRAFT in POUNDS PER FOOT OF IMPLEMENT WIDTH

Here is a selection guide that shows approximate drafts of several types of tined soil-working equipment.

avoiding overapplication and drift. Excellent information on calibrating and using spreaders and sprayers can be found on www.lsuagcenter.com, the website of Louisiana State University (LSU).

ALTERNATIVES TO CHEMICAL SPRAYS

There are interesting alternative pest control possibilities that are environmentally friendly and should be considered. These include the use of crop or grazing animal rotations, weed shading by crops, biological agents, hot-water applicators for orchards and paved-area weed control, and flame or thermal weeding. There are no residues or drift problems with flaming, which is pesticide-free and it is highly cost competitive with herbicide application. Flame weeders are available in all sizes from portable wands to broad-acre units. Alfalfa flaming is designed to kill weeds and the alfalfa weevil. Go to www.flameengineering.com for examples.

GENERATORS/GENSETS

Recent calamities on the coastal areas and the regular northern winter windstorms remind us of the value of having a generator to power at least part of the home in an emergency. Generators are also valuable for powering electric tools at sites distant from power outlets. The great advantage of having a tractor-PTO generator is that you don't need an extra engine, and you get a lot more bang for your buck from the tractor compared with what it would cost to get the same kilowatts from a separate engine-powered genset. Briggs & Stratton recently launched a clever 120-volt AC generator design that is built into the engine housing. The system has automatic overload protection, double receptacle, and ground-fault circuit interruptor. For example, a suitably equipped, 18-horsepower Deere GT 325e

A riding tractor with Briggs & Stratton PowerLink system converts electricity generated by the engine into a kilowatt of usable AC power. Briggs & Stratton ELS V-Twin and Vanguard engines with PowerLink are available on several Craftsman and John Deere riding-mower models. Briggs & Stratton

Kubota L30 with FEL and 3PL rotary hoe is shown here at work. Kubota

These pages and following: Kubota tractors are versitile and can be used to pull many implements. Kubota

garden tractor with the Briggs PowerLink unit can generate one kilowatt continuous or 1.5-kw surge on demand.

Safety alert with a generator: It is essential to use a utility-approved, double-pole transfer switch and correct installation before plugging your mobile generator into the household switchboard. Other people's lives and the generator are at risk if those measures are not taken.

Compact Equipment magazine's publishers offer an annual attachment buyer's guide (ABG), which is a resource for navigating the attachment industry, especially in an environment where the attachment industry is growing but fragmented. This guide is geared toward the owner-operator of compact equipment needing to find attachments for any of these five tool carriers: skid steers/track loaders, compact excavators, compact utility loaders (also called mini-skid steers), compact tractors, and utility vehicles.

Bobcat

112

Bobcat

Bobcat

Bobcat

Flame weeders are drift- and residue-free means of weed control. Even some pests are also amenable to control by flaming. Flameengineering.com

CHAPTER 8
TRACTOR AND SYSTEM PERFORMANCE

Testing a tractor or powered piece of equipment on the job before buying is usually not feasible. Prospective tractor buyers and managers need to have some way to assess performance beforehand and predict the system's work capabilities. In some instances, information may be available from formal testing agencies, such as the Nebraska Tractor Test Laboratory. Other than that, manufacturer's literature, published articles, and state extension services are helpful. Finally, there is word of mouth from dealers and owners of similar outfits.

This book lays out some basic principles for predicting performance, and after you have the machine or system, getting

This Kubota model M105 has a bale spear and pallet-fork bale carriers on each end. Kubota

Productivity for this Kubota model 2630 with TLB combination is measured by how many feet of trench can be dug in a day. Kubota

the best out of it. However, before considering the prime mover there is the decision about what it will be used for and what attachments or implements will it be equipped with.

Once the tractor/attachment/implement system is specified, there are four ways to assess performance of the system:

1. Field and Pattern Performance
2. Power Performance
3. Quality Performance
4. Operator Performance

Each of these plays into the overall economics of the system and the cost effectiveness of or return on investment from a job.

FIELD PERFORMANCE

You can rapidly calculate how big an acreage you can cover with the field capacity (FC) rule.

Acres an Hour = Implement Width (feet) x Speed (miles per hour) ÷ 10

This is the field capacity of any piece of equipment of given width with the tractor operated at the selected speed. Strictly speaking, the divisor in U.S. units is 8.25, but making it 10 allows for time lost in turns, operator breaks, etc., which is a time loss of about 17.5 percent short of the theoretical capacity. In metric units, theoretical FC is Hectares an Hour = Width (meters) x Speed (kilometers per hour) ÷ 10.

According to this rule a wider and faster machine will

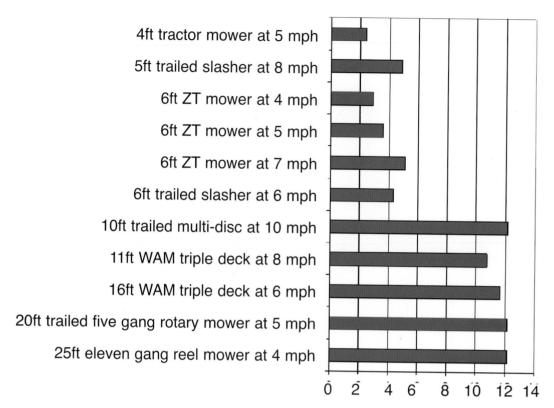

4ft tractor mower at 5 mph
5ft trailed slasher at 8 mph
6ft ZT mower at 4 mph
6ft ZT mower at 5 mph
6ft ZT mower at 7 mph
6ft trailed slasher at 6 mph
10ft trailed multi-disc at 10 mph
11ft WAM triple deck at 8 mph
16ft WAM triple deck at 6 mph
20ft trailed five gang rotary mower at 5 mph
25ft eleven gang reel mower at 4 mph

0 2 4 6 8 10 12 14

When mowing, increasing speed does not necessarily result in a proportional increase in mowing rate in practice because you still have to turn at the ends of the run and maneuver around trees and obstacles. Nonproductive time becomes a larger percentage of total time as your speed increases and on shorter straights. Increasing deck width might require a lower forward speed and negate the effect of a wider mower.

have the higher FC unless there are conditions that would interfere with straightforward work. If a high level of maneuverability is essential, then a zero-turn with a narrow deck may outperform a wider, conventional ride-on mower.

Actual field performance falls short if it is less than the Theoretical by the Field Efficiency Factor:

Field Efficiency (FE) = $\dfrac{\text{Actual Field Capacity} \times 100}{\text{Theoretical Field Capacity}}$

Some notional FE figures:

Mowing   FE = 80 to 90 percent
Cultivating   FE = 68 to 80 percent
Spraying   FE = 55 to 80 percent
Earthmoving FE = 80 percent

Another way to calculate the field capacity is:

Actual Field Capacity (AFC) = Theoretical FC x Field Efficiency

Material capacity is relevant to such activities as moving dirt, baling hay, or harvesting:

Tons of Product per Hour = Yield (tons/acre) x AFC (acres/hour)
Productivity = Load per Cycle x Cycles per Hour
Unit Cost in Dollars per Ton = Dollars per Hour ÷ Tons per Hour

PATTERN PERFORMANCE

Closely connected with field efficiency is pattern performance or efficiency. There are many ways that you can work over an area. Will you go round and round or up and down? What about turning at the corners? At least eight patterns are used in broadacre farming and most of them are pertinent to compact equipment operations. There are ideas there that you can use to more effectively work an area. Determining the best pattern will be governed by:

How sharp can you turn with the implement?

Can the implement be left down in working mode while cornering, or does it need to be raised at the corners?

Will sharp cornering cause scuffing or gouging of the surface?

Is there space for executing turns?

Do you need to dump material (like clippings or hay bales) at the end of each row?

If so, is there a single dump site, or several en route?

For turf, do you need to leave a striping pattern on the greens' surface or do you specifically want to avoid striping?

How uniform does the finish need to be?

Will overlapping cause problems (as it can with chemical application)?

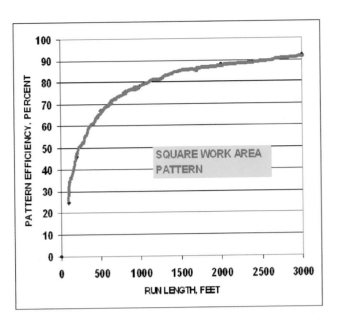

This chart shows the effect of field length on pattern efficiency for square worked areas. The less time spent turning the better. This data applies only to a square area of length specified.

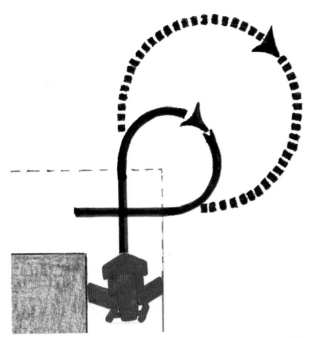

Continuous-loop turn pattern. Ninety-degree loop turns eliminate unprocessed pieces of the field but consume time. The solid line shows a turn if turning brakes were used. The dotted line is without using turning brakes.

Certain field patterns are more time efficient than others, particularly those that execute the fastest turns, but the greatest influence on pattern efficiency is the shape of the field. The highest pattern efficiency would be achieved if the field was extremely long, straight, and narrow for a given area, as compared with the same area that was squat, triangular, or irregular.

Pattern is a key issue when lawn or turf mowing. Mowing repeatedly in an identical pattern results in wheel marks and ugly stripes, especially if the turf is driven on when damp. To remedy that, vary the mowing pattern. That will minimize tire marks and ruts because the tires will run in different places each time. An additional benefit is that alternate or varying patterns can be very attractive and, done the right way, the area can take on a pleasing checkerboard appearance. Greens (lawns, fairways, sports fields) will take somewhat longer to mow in the less-efficient patterns, but the results can be well worth the appearance.

Circuitous patterns are sometimes called racecourse or round and round. Driving in circles is simple enough, but how about the corners? The two simplest types of turns on a rectangular course are 90-degree continuous and loop turns. The 90-degree turns are plain no-nonsense turns but they leave crescent-shaped pieces unworked. Doing a loop turn at each corner on the other hand makes a neat cusp and cuts out the corners at each turn so that no further work is needed there. The penalty is turn time, which can eat up useful work time, especially in a short field.

There are several other types of fancy turns that are possible but are more complex and time consuming, They also depend on factors such as whether the attachment is towed or front mounted and whether there is a fixed operating pattern needed, as there is with a side-mounted sickle bar mower or a moldboard plow that throws to one side. Turning consumes a lot of otherwise productive time.

What is the price paid in time for turns? The first thing to consider is the length of the field. In a 250-acre field that is exactly square, continuous 90-degree turns would take approximately 8 percent of the time (pattern efficiency about 92 percent). In a square field of 2 1/2 acres, 29 percent of the time would be absorbed by the 90-degree turns. In a 1-acre square field, 46 percent of the time would be consumed by turning, and that's just working in circles. If you were to do loop turns at the corners on a 1-acre area, that could jump to as much as 70 percent of the time spent in turns.

Working lands and headland patterns is another pattern type. Working lands refers to the practice of dividing an area or a field that has straight sides into sub-areas and individually working those sub-areas. That will inevitably call for space to execute the continuous 180-degree turns at the end of each trip. Those turn-strips are headlands, which will need subsequent processing to tidy up. Headland pattern work is more interesting/challenging for the operator than going in circles! For turf striping a sports field, premeditated headland working leaves a nice pattern. The

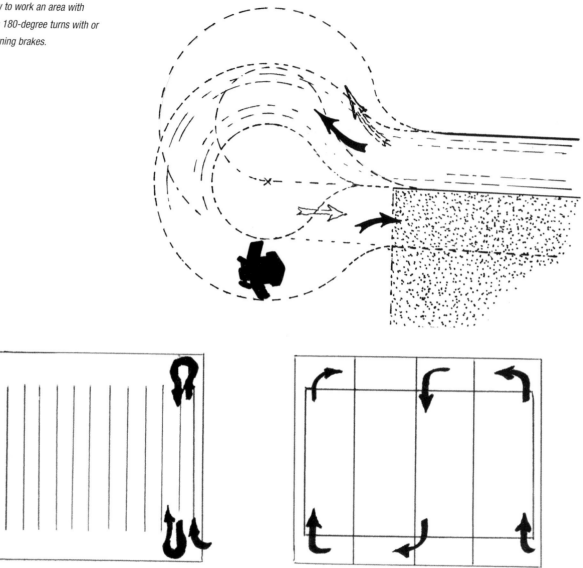

Here is an example of working backwards and forwards from the boundaries inwards with 180-degree turns (left) or working in lands (right).

wider the lands, the greater the pattern efficiency. There are several variants on working in lands and turn patterns that have their own advantages and drawbacks, but to go into these in detail would take more space than is available here.

POWER PERFORMANCE

Power performance is measured by the mechanical efficiency of powered mobile equipment to deliver power from the engine flywheel down to where it's needed—to the ground or through PTOs or hydraulic outlets. As mentioned in Chapter 4, a tractor can deliver up to 90 percent of engine power at the PTO and around 80 percent out of hydraulics if that was all the tractor was driving. In reality, most tractor work is done on-the-go, so that

brings the focus on traction and how much power can be delivered to the ground.

If you're working on rough, undulating ground, like towing a trailed brush hog or rotavating on the back 40, you better have ample power to be able to push on over the hills and drive the implement. Where traction—the ability to develop drawbar pull—is concerned, tire selection and management is important. But there is more to consider. Drawbar power is affected by ground-drive system and gearing, wheel ballasting, hitch placement, and tire configuration. These all contribute to the tractor's pulling ability.

Tractor tires are either lugged or nonlugged. The lugs are for traction and should always be mounted with the V-pattern pointing downwards at the front of a traction tire. Tractor drive

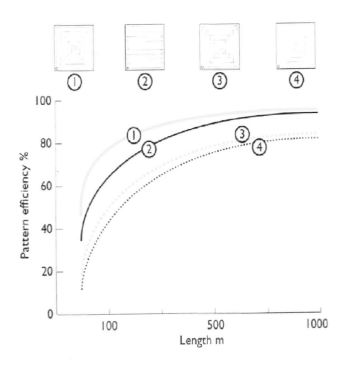

Some field operating patterns and comparing pattern efficiency are shown here.

tires are designated with an R prefix. Nondriving front tires are often ribbed to aid steering and are designated by an F prefix. The off-road tires are distinguished by an E prefix.

Tires have either biased ply or radial ply inside the rubber shell. The number of plies inside the tire dictate the load rating and service work the tire can withstand. Skid-steer loaders and stake-proof forestry tractors are equipped with tires with as many as 16 plies. Radials can be operated at lower tire pressures, which give better traction and a softer ride, but they cost more. Tire traction depends on the weight on the tire and soil conditions. The load the tire can carry in turn is governed by the tire pressure and speed, which have certain limits that are usually inscribed on the tire. A certain amount of slippage is necessary for any traction and pull. For wheeled tractors on drawbar work, it could be around 12 to 15 percent wheel slip, but only 3 percent slip for rubber tracks. Ballasting the tires or tractor for optimal drawbar pull and balance is complex. For example, there is a different ballast for roadwork than for fieldwork. Surface compaction and marking of greens are frequently areas of concern. For those reasons special flotation tires and tread patterns are available for greens-keeping tractors.

QUALITY PERFORMANCE

In a farm processing operation, quality usually refers to the standard of grain, fruit, or hay produced in the operation. For tractor systems work, in addition to those product-quality considerations, there are two other facets to the tractor systems' quality performance: the job that the attachments do or what sort of finish they leave and the reliability of the tractor and attachments to complete the job.

Mowing finish can be measured by the appearance of the turf after the passage of the mower. Is there any scalping or unevenness of cut? How about striping? What about the headlands after cultivating?

Tractor reliability depends on whether the machine is new or used, initial tractor quality out of the factory (for new machines), how many hours are on the meter, how the tractor and attachments are used or abused in service, and how faithfully service and maintenance are managed in order to keep the machine system operable with minimum downtime. Breakdowns are inevitable sooner or later. The probability and extent of a breakdown is a combination of many factors, including the operator.

OPERATOR PERFORMANCE

A businessman might manage an operation with considerable skill and knowledge about machine performance. But with a careless or inexperienced driver on the machine, overall system performance will be low and profitability will suffer. A compact equipment manager has certain obligations by law to provide the safest reasonable environment and employee training in effective use and safety. Tractors and machines are dangerous. A long day's work behind the wheel, the noise, and the need to be constantly alert is fatiguing, apart from any physical effort involved.

Modern compact tractors have sophisticated controls. The more complex, the greater the need for sharpness, knowledge, and skill in operation. A person might be able to drive a mini-excavator, backhoe, or front-end loader, but no one could operate effectively without some introduction to the controls. There's a difference between a driver and an operator! Just how skillful an operator will become depends so much on ability, experience, training, motivation, aptitude, health, and alertness.

Field efficiency is of necessity always less than 100 percent due to operator factors and delays but those delays are essential repair, maintenance, and machine-servicing delays or time idled or lost by the operator. The operator's work organization is the final factor in the efficiency equation.

ERGONOMICS AND OPERATOR PERFORMANCE FACTORS

A comfortable tractor will enable the operator to stay at it for more hours in the day. Ergonomics has to do broadly with comfort and the operator's platform and controls layout,

A Kubota L30 operator sees a digital display that shows which operating mode is functional at the time. Kubota

lowest reasonable noise and vibration levels, facility with the controls, operator perceptions and peer pressure, work organization, and implementing safe work practices. Look for ergonomically designed tractor features and use them to operate effectively and safely.

EFFECTIVE TRACTOR-DRIVING SKILLS

Good driving experience will never come from a book. The best this segment can do is add a few tips to what is already available in quality tractor owner manuals:

Always sit in the driver's seat when starting or working the tractor. Never leave the seat with equipment running.

Don't be in a rush with tractor work. Treat the machine like you would if handed a drowsy snake. It can be lethal if mishandled. Watch where you are going at all times.

Keep the tractor in gear going downhill. Start down in low gear to use the engine as a brake. Don't attempt to change gears midway down with a conventional gearbox transmission.

If you ever get bogged, back out to prevent backflipping the tractor.

On geared tractors, engage clutch gradually.

To save fuel, don't allow a gasoline-powered tractor to stand and idle for prolonged periods. Switch off the engine if lengthy delays are expected.

Avoid letting the fuel tank run dry. It can cause fuel system problems and require repairs due to crud in the bottom of the tank and lead to possible fuel pump damage or blockages.

Running out of fuel is even more of a problem for diesels, where the injection system needs fuel for lubrication. After running out of fuel, most diesel systems need the fuel system bled to remove air before the engine can be restarted.

Use implement-to-tractor weight transfer where possible for improved traction.

Avoid prolonged heavy pulling work in the lowest gears. It can shorten tractor transmission life.

Gear up and throttle back for best fuel economy.

Thoroughly read the operator's manual. There is much wisdom in there.

CHAPTER 9
COMPACT TRACTOR AND EQUIPMENT SAFETY

ACCIDENT FACTS

Garden tractors cause 45 deaths and nearly 50,000 injuries per year in the United States. Although the numbers have been declining over the past decade, those numbers for garden tractors and the many more caused by larger tractors are still horrible statistics.

An accident is an unforeseen event, but it can be prevented. The cause of most accidents can be traced back, which makes an accident statistically predictable. Often the cause is impulsive, careless, or overconfident behavior. The power and speed of the machines today make even a moment's distraction dangerous. Evidence is mounting that 20 percent of road accidents are caused by driver fatigue. It's likely that the same factors are at work in tractor accidents.

It's trite to say that accidents occur fast. If that wasn't the case, operators would have time to take evasive action. Since accidents do take place fast and unexpectedly, the safe course is to identify hazards, control those you can do something about, and be in a state of alertness to things outside your control.

Accident prevention is a combination of engineering design, education, and regulatory enforcement. Designs for improved safety have moved along greatly since the days when tractors were hand cranked. Regulations have limited application since most tractors are operated by independent individuals where there are no supervisors to enforce rules, which leaves education and a knowledge base on safety to be elaborated here.

Exmark is voluntarily installing ROPS at the factory on its zero-turn mowers.
Hustler Turf Equipment

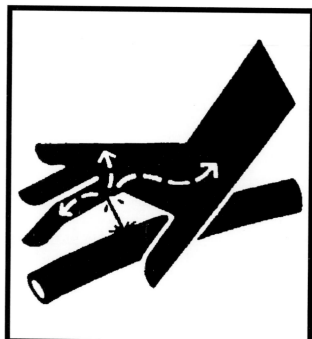

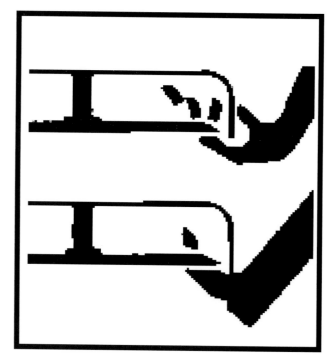

ASAE and SAE have a series of representational pictorials to explicitly indicate hazards around machines. ASAE Standard S434

Avoiding accidents with tractors means approaching tractor work with an attitude for safety. Safety begins with concentrating on the task at hand, even before climbing on the tractor. Proactive safety management is no accident! Safety management influences the bottom line. A safe attitude includes knowing that accidents have consequences. Safety is an attitude. Think ahead, think safety.

SAFETY KNOW-HOW

There are four steps in proactive accident prevention: identify hazards, assess risks, control the risks, and constantly review the hazards. Employers have certain responsibilities that are regulated. The Occupational Safety and Health Administration (OSHA) requires that tractors over 20 horsepower and manufactured after October 1976 that are used by employees be equipped with ROPS and seat belts. Employees also need to be instructed about hazards and protected from sharp surfaces, and spillage of tractor fluids. To maintain safety features, employers and operators should:

• Read and understand the operator's manual before using any machine.
• Get to know the equipment and keep it in safe condition.
• Adhere to proper maintenance schedules.
• Conduct preoperation checks.
• Ensure that safety interlocks are functional.
• Maintain safety decals including the slow moving vehicle (SMV) emblem.
• Refuel sensibly.
• Keep a 20-pound ABC fire extinguisher at the workplace.
• Minimize hazards, check that all shields are in place, and keep out of harm's way.
• Wear sensible clothing when working with tractors and equipment. Wear pants, steel-toed boots, goggles, and

WHAT ARE THE CONSEQUENCES OF AN ACCIDENT?

The personal consequences of a machinery accident causing injury are in increasing order of importance:

- Pain and inconvenience
- Work delays
- Lost production
- Loss of livelihood
- Economic (and property) losses and costs
- More paperwork, potential liability claims, higher insurance premiums
- Disablement and pain
- Injuries from accidents, impacts on the hurt individual, the family, and others
- Death

ear protection. No bare feet, sandals, tennis shoes, or slippery footwear of any kind. No hanging jewelry should be worn. Secure long hair. Clothing should fit closely because loose-fitting clothing can be deadly around rotating parts. Skimpy clothes give no protection from burns or projectiles traveling at 200 miles per hour, which is the muzzle velocity at a mower's discharge zone.

- Never attempt to make adjustments or repairs to the tractor or attachments while the engine is running. Only trained personnel should perform repairs or maintenance requiring engine power.
- Never work under the machine unless it is securely supported with stands, blocks, or a hoist.
- Be aware of the machine's potential hot parts.
- Don't leave the seat with equipment still running.
- Never leave the machines running and unattended.
- Never run engines in an enclosed area unless the exhaust is vented directly to the outside. Carbon monoxide is odorless and deadly poisonous.
- High-speed rotating equipment, such as mowers, slashers, and mulchers, have blades rotating at speeds up to 200 miles per hour. Keep clear of moving blades and ensure all shields, guards, and chains are in place to keep your anatomy out of the danger zone and prevent injury from thrown objects. People have been injured or killed inside cabs by objects thrown up by slashers and ricocheted from chassis components.
- Be wary around any machine that stores energy. Maintain all guards and shields in place.
- Observe all traffic laws when on public roads. Use legal lighting and signals.

THE TWO MOST COMMON TRACTOR ACCIDENTS

The most frequent cause of death and injury with tractors is sideways rollovers. About 50 percent of tractor accidents involve rollovers. Tractors are not as stable as autos and have a narrower and shorter wheelbase, a higher center of gravity, and a much greater weight-to-power ratio than cars. A 900-horsepower Monte Carlo racing car with an extremely low center of gravity weighs just over half a ton, which is about the same weight as a 25-horsepower compact tractor! Tractors generally have a pivoting front axle that narrows the initial tipping zone.

A mower facing uphill or a tractor with a heavy drawbar loading is like a loaded gun with the safety catch off. If the operator's foot slips off the clutch at full revs, the machine can rear up and over in less than two seconds. Always release the clutch gradually, even on flat land. Never pull from anywhere else than the drawbar when driving forward. If the anticipated load is very heavy, pull in reverse from an appropriate front attachment point. A more subtle danger is rough terrain. Don't depend on a rear-mounted 3PL implement to prevent a tractor from backflipping.

Correct ballasting will not only improve tractor productivity, but also reduce tipping hazards. Heavy mounted equipment front or rear requires corresponding ballast at the opposite end of the tractor. Suitcase weights on a bracket are the usual weight on the front. For tractors with front loaders and no regular implement on the rear, a weight bracket or a concrete weight with pins for the three-point hitch provides balance.

Rollover protective system design standards that were first published in 1967 eventually resulted in OSHA requirements that employers must ensure that all tractors of more than 20 horsepower be fitted with a ROPS, have a seat belt that meets the requirements of SAE Standard J4C, and ensure that each employee uses the seat belt and tightens the belt sufficiently to confine the employee within the ROPS.

ROPS provide a safe enclosure zone, and seat belts hold drivers in that zone. ROPS and seat belts together can prevent 99 percent of deaths from tractor overturns. The problem is that ROPS are still not fitted to a large number of tractors, such as older models and smaller tractors like tractor-mowers. A home-built frame cannot ensure safety. (See ASAE Standard S383.1 for further information.)

Manufacturers have been voluntarily fitting ROPS on all tractors sold over 30 horsepower since 1985. Exmark has gone further to ensure that its entire line of Lazer Z, mid-mount zero-turn riding mowers, despite being lower than 30 horsepower, can come equipped with ROPS, including

When moving forward, never hitch a load from anywhere other than the manufacturer's drawbar.

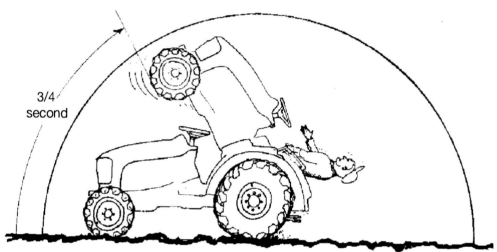

A tractor can flip over backwards in less than two seconds in the wrong circumstance.

3/4 second

some with a fold-down feature to facilitate easy on/off trailer loading, as well as mowing around low tree limbs.

The full height of a ROPS can be an inconvenience in certain types of work. Foldable ROPS are available. The seatbelt should not be worn with a folded ROPS since the ROPS is ineffective in that position. Always secure the ROPS in the upright position as soon as possible when close clearance work is done.

OTHER HAZARDOUS TRACTOR SITUATIONS

Bouncing and tractor hop can cause loss of steering control. Tractor hopping is affected by the way a tractor is balanced and its tire configuration. A 3PL heavy-duty slasher mounted on back is enough to cause loss of control if driven at speed over bumpy ground if the machine is not ballasted up front. Correct air pressures and radial tires are instrumental in reducing tractor hop. See Chapter 4 for ideal weight distribution on tractors.

Once in motion, all bodies have momentum. Be on guard against the tractor being pushed into a dangerous

situation by implement inertia. This applies to the way the clutch is released at full engine speed and equally to PTO-driven equipment. For example, the tractor can surge forward unexpectedly by an over-running, heavy-duty mower, even when the clutch is depressed. An over-running clutch option would reduce that hazard.

Never carry riders on tractors or riding mowers. The only exceptions are some European tractors equipped with a buddy seat and ROPS. A seatbelt must be used at all times with the buddy seat.

Falls from tractors are due to unsafe or improper mounting and dismounting. An operator should always face the tractor when going up or down the steps where the handholds are in position to be used. Many falls from a tractor result in injury or death. A rear wheel is so close and ready to fatally crush a fallen extra rider.

Tractor runovers happen when the driver can't see children or others in the line of travel; a rider falls from the steps, cab, or drawbar; when traversing rough ground or reversing; or bypass starting. All of these accidents are preventable with sensible operation. Never get off a moving

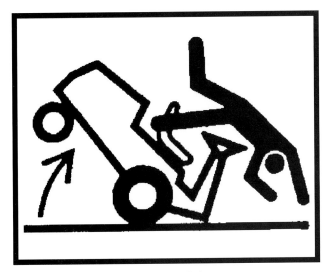

A riding mower can also be tipped if mishandled.

Individuals are run over and killed by tractors every year.

Watch out for children when operating large equipment. They tend to be fascinated by machines. Take extreme care that children are not anywhere near, especially when moving in reverse. ASAE Standard S434

tractor or leave it with its engine running. Shut down any attachments before leaving the seat. A runaway tractor is extremely dangerous.

An assistant can be crushed between a tractor and a machine being attached. That can happen due to a breakdown of communication or loss of control; the worker on the ground is in the wrong spot, the tractor moves rearward too much, or the tractor operator cannot see the worker, who is then crushed between the machines. To prevent crushing accidents, the assistant should never enter the area between the tractor and the attachment until the tractor has

been stopped, shifted into neutral, and the brakes engaged. Keep the worker out of the hazardous area if adjustments have to be made between the tractor and the machine. The area between the front and rear wheels on either side of many articulated tractors is a danger zone. Movement of the steering wheel brings the front and rear chassis closer with more than enough power to crush someone.

Look around and disengage powered equipment before backing up. Never uncouple the electrical connectors of a built-in seat switch or reversing controller. John Deere is one of the companies that has a reverse implement option

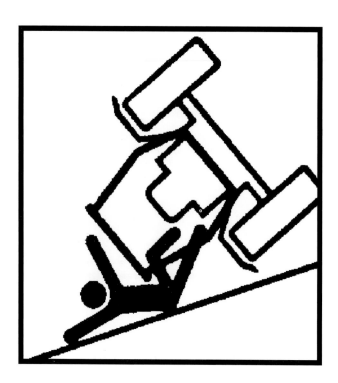

Tractors are not very stable on slopes.

Mower blades can hurl objects for great distances and with destructive force.

This is a severely injured limb from entanglement with a PTO-driven auger.

(RIO) on all 1999 and later John Deere and Sabre riding mowers and garden tractors. As John Deere's booklet aptly states: "If you should forget to look behind, you will appreciate the benefits of RIO because the attached mower or implement will shut off automatically as a protection against a moment's thoughtlessness." With John Deere's system, you need to engage a switch if you want to keep the equipment operating when moving backwards, so it's a built-in safety reminder.

Starting a tractor while standing on the ground beside the machine is never a safe procedure. To do this, the operator must either make electrical connections on the starter motor or reach up and over to turn the ignition key. An operator standing on the ground cannot be sure if the transmission is in neutral or park. If a manual transmission is in gear when the engine is bypass started, the tractor can run over the operator. There may be a slight delay if the tractor has a hydrostatic transmission or power-shift transmission, but the delay is insufficient for the victim to escape.

Children often aren't mature enough or sufficiently coordinated to drive tractors, hitch tractor attachments, or properly assess hazardous situations. Don't let them near or allow them to operate tractors.

WORKING SLOPES

"Two things a tractor's good for: It can put up a little hay for you, and it can turn over on a hillside and kill you."—North Carolina farmer John Dale, who spurns tractors to continue farming with mules. (Cited in National Geographic, March 1980: 346.)

Hillsides and steeply undulating land pose extra tractor hazards for compact tractors and mowers on slopes. The relatively high center of gravity and a narrow wheelbase makes tractors top heavy compared with an auto. Add to that the tractor's higher pulling effort in low gear and it means that tractors can readily become unstable. Even on flat ground, gopher holes or rapid swerving can precipitate an accident. As one wit has put it, "If it feels dangerous, it probably is," and "It doesn't need to feel dangerous to be dangerous."

There are many safety issues you must consider before mowing hillsides or uneven ground. The tractor must have a roll bar or ROPS and seat belt. If you own a old tractor

PTO shields are essential. Loose clothing can quickly get caught in revolving machine components.

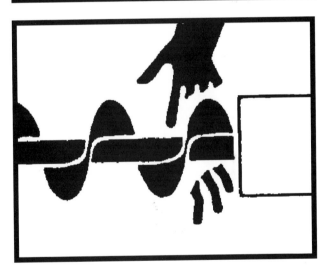

This is a hand that was pinched in a rotating machine component.

or mowing tractor without ROPS, don't even contemplate driving on sloping land until you get a ROPS!

If wheel-track width is adjustable, use the widest possible setting. Dual wheels can enhance sidehill stability considerably. If you're contemplating a tractor purchase for hilly land, a front-wheel-drive tractor is a somewhat safer option. Use suitable wheel weights or calcium solution in tires that are inflated to the appropriate pressure to improve tractor balance, traction, and stability. A heavy trailed implement or trailer can upset a tractor's balance. Use a rolling hitch for heavy-duty equipment.

Clear the slopes of as many obstructions, such as debris and rocks, and if it is slippery wait until the area has dried out. Never mow a hillside when it is wet. Hidden obstacles can rapidly change the tractor's equilibrium. Proceed slowly and cautiously at all times, and avoid as much as possible driving into ditches or along steep embankments.

Start gradually going uphill. Tractors can backflip going uphill, especially with a rear implement or when towing. Travel directly up or down a hill, not across the slope. If you end up on a side slope, always turn down the hill and with the slope, not into the slope. If you have to tow a hefty load uphill, attach the load to an appropriate place on the front of the tractor and move up the hill in reverse. Likewise, when pulling out a stubborn tree stump, pull from the front, not the rear. Pull loads only from the drawbar when driving forward and never use elastic or nylon haul ropes for heavy pulling. When towing a load downhill, use a low gear and use low-idle engine braking. Don't attempt to shift manual gears or declutch on the way down, you may not be able to get the tractor back into gear in an emergency. If anything causes a loss of traction, cautiously drive off the slope immediately. Determine the cause of the lost traction and resolve the problem before resuming slope work.

Before you mow on a slope, there are some considerations and alternatives to keep in mind. Consider purpose-built equipment designed for safely mowing on slopes (see Chapter 5). Trailed mowers may be useful for steep berms or other hard-to-reach places. Proceed with extra caution and work up and down the slope, not sideways, and across the slope as far as possible. An articulated boom mower is the safest way to groom ditch banks, gullies, and undulating road verges, but it requires specific hydraulics on the tractor. (Bomford's Micro-Mower is shown in Chapter 5.) Several companies have demonstrated remote-controlled mowers. The

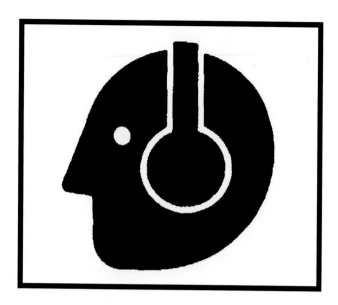

Hearing protection can be provided by earplugs or earmuffs and by distancing yourself from the source of sound.

mowers spin at up to 3,000 rpm. If a foot gets in the way at that speed, the blades can take 20 bites out of the appendage before a person reacts and pulls back. The blades can be traveling at top speeds of 200 miles per hour and have enough energy to hurl objects as far as 50 feet.

If the mower hits something, stop the machine to inspect the unit and repair any damage before resuming. Disconnect the spark plug lead before attempting to unclog a chute or perform any sort of maintenance work. Always use a tool—not your hand—for removing mower slugs.

All shut-off mechanisms, such as seat switches, should be fully operational. Removal of such devices is far too common, and while their elimination might seem to simplify or accelerate the mower's operation, the consequences can be catastrophic.

Never carry riders. Always mow alone. Do not mow in reverse unless it is absolutely necessary. If you must mow in reverse, stop before shifting, then watch behind you the entire time you are moving. Children are not machine savvy. Keep children completely away from the machine.

operator controlling the mower by radio stands in a safe location away from the mower.

An alternative for slopes is to plant a ground cover. Vetiver or Mondo grass or spreading shrubs that don't need regular attention or mowing are sensible options. Deploy livestock, such as sheep or goats, to keep the hillside trimmed—but fence them in!

You can also hire a contractor to mow the hillside. Professionals often have commercial equipment designed for hillside mowing.

On any terrain, be careful when mowing around large shrubs or trees with limbs hanging at eye level because they are dangerous for eyes and face trauma. You also want to be careful around the mower blades. The blades on rotary

Never leave an unattended machine running. Always disengage the mower; set the parking brake, and stop the engine before dismounting or removing a grass collector. Watch traffic when crossing or operating near roadways. Watch for holes, ruts, bumps, or other uneven terrain that could overturn the mower.

Tractor brakes can be worn or inadequate with heavy trailed equipment on back. Traveling downhill calls for extra care. Before heading downhill, be sure to engage a low gear that can hold the machine back without being

JCB's tracked Robot Loader at work. JCB Sales Limited

dependent on the brakes. Stay in gear, don't depress the clutch, and take your time. Be concerned about jack-knifing while going downhill with trailed equipment. It is better to work up and down a slope rather than across the slope. Side rollovers are caused if one wheel suddenly drops into a pothole or slides off the side of an embankment. You also need to be careful when traveling at speed. A sudden swerve can lead to disaster due to the tractor's high center of gravity, especially if you are towing a heavy trailed load.

Mandatory (and sensible) shielding around PTOs can be inconvenient and get in the way when connecting or disconnecting the drivelines. If a shield or guard has to be moved, don't be tempted to leave the shields off. Replace shields or guards immediately after any changes. Make sure the shaft shields can rotate freely, but that the shaft shields are properly restrained. Always be wary around any rotating mechanisms. PTO stub shafts and any rotating machine elements may grab loose clothing, and entanglement causes severe injuries. Also watch out for drives with pinch points, such as exposed pulleys, gears, or levers. Don't trust the machine—treat it like you would handle a drowsy snake!

HAZARDS WITH HYDRAULICS

Modern tractors, mowers, and loaders are often mobile hydraulic power packs. Maintenance and repair of their hydraulic systems call for a cautious approach. Any hydraulic fluid that escapes under pressure can penetrate the skin. Mineral hydraulic fluids can also infect minor cuts or scratches. Any wounds exposed to hydraulic fluid need medical attention.

Before applying pressure to a hydraulic system, ensure that all connections are tight and all hoses and lines are in good condition. Relieve all pressure in the system before disconnecting or working on hydraulic lines. To find a leak under pressure, expose a piece of cardboard or wood to the line; never test with your body.

FRONT-END LOADER SAFETY

Before moving a front-end loader (FEL), look 360 degrees around you to make sure no one is in your path. Never carry any riders. A loader with a full bucket has an entirely different center of gravity. Without a load, the rear of the loader carries the weight; with a load, the front of the loader is heaviest. Travel up and down slopes with the heavy end of the loader pointed uphill; keep the lift arms down and the bucket tilted up. If you cannot avoid a steep slope, travel straight up or down the slope, never across it. If obstacles or ditches are unavoidable, reduce speed, raise the bucket to clear the ground, and cross at an angle. Keep away from dropoffs and never operate too close to an overhang or gully. Be alert to the danger of an unrestrained round bale rolling down the raised loader arms. More than one operator has had his back broken as a result. Keep the lift arms down when traveling or turning. Be wary around loaders with raised buckets or 3PL lift arms. Lower the equipment at the end of any job. To load the FEL on a trailer, drive up the ramp with the heavy end pointing uphill. Lower the bucket so it rests on the trailer bed and secure the loader adequately with tie downs at front and rear.

FATIGUE IS A CONTRIBUTOR TO ACCIDENTS

Serious tractor work involves long hours on jobs including mowing, skid-steer loading, or cultivating. The jolting around on a full day's work is tiring, especially on short wheelbase machines like a skid steer. A tractor with a hand throttle doesn't stop if you fall asleep at the wheel. Diesel

Walsh-Healey Act/OSHA Tolerable Noise Levels:

Duration Per Day (hours)	Sound Level (dBA scale)
.25	115
.5	110
1	105
3	100
3	97
4	95
6	92
8	90

Note: A Walkman does not count for hearing protection. In fact, the distraction of headphones may prevent an operator from hearing a dangerous situation and add decibels to an already noisy environment.

engines are loud, and noise causes fatigue and inattention, which leads to accidents. Fatigue plus alcohol or other drugs is a deadly mix for an operator.

How noisy is your work environment? Inexpensive meters are available today that measure sound intensity in decibels (dB), a logarithmic sound pressure scale. For every 3 dB rise in the reading, the sound pressure has doubled. Note that a sharply painful sound of 140 dB (like the noise of a close shotgun blast) is 10 million times as loud as the least discernible sound level. The A-scale is the register commonly used around machinery. If your workplace involves exposures to levels higher than these tabled below for the durations listed, you will suffer hearing damage. Some means of approved hearing protection is essential, such as shielding the ears with muffs or earplugs, distancing yourself from the noise source, and reducing exposure duration.

To put these numbers into perspective, a remote wilderness area may have an ambient reading of 35 dBA; the sound of a moderate rainfall is 50 dBA; normal conversation is 60 dBA; traffic is 60 to 75 dBA; a lawnmower is 90 dBA; an angle grinder is 97 dBA; an idling chain saw is 100 dBA with 110 dBA when cutting at full throttle, which also happens to be the noise level of a rock band. The exhaust note on an old powerful tractor can reach 100 dBA at ear level, but the noise inside the cab of modern tractors may be 73 dBA. Mower decks are noisy and almost as loud as the machine's exhaust note.

CHAPTER 10
CALCULATING OWNING AND OPERATING COSTS

Around 160,000 compact tractors and 100,000 riding mowers are sold annually in the United States and the demand is not decreasing. One of the many reasons for the healthy demand for these machines is the aging population. Retirees often have more discretionary spending power, and with an affinity for the outdoors, small tractors are appealing for their estates, acreage, or hobby farms. Apart from retirees, there is a movement of people wanting to live a rural lifestyle. Even if their lot size is a fraction of an acre, give them a bit of space and their imagination can do the rest. Those neat and versatile small tractors have a lot of appeal, and what's a farm without a tractor? This chapter intends to show you (hopefully without putting you off) that there is a lot more to buying than the first cost!

A farm tractor may use 50 percent of its initial cost on service, repairs, and maintenance (R&M) over five years. Construction equipment might even run up R&M costs of up to 100 percent over a working life. Granted a noncommercial tractor will not log as many hours as a farm tractor, but right from the outset there are still R&M costs to be aware of. The matter of life (hours on the meter) is vital in any costs calculations.

TRACTOR LONGEVITY

How long a tractor will last is hard to pin down. Collectors of vintage tractors have some cosseted beauties that have been kept for more than a century and are still operable. For example, there are several 1903 Ivels still running. There are also thousands of intact John Deere Model A Johnny Poppers out there with half a century on the clock. Tractor longevity varies greatly, depending on original machine quality and how the machine is used and serviced. Estimating the life of a machine, or how long you will hang onto it, is critically important in calculating owning and operating costs. OPEI pegs the life of rear-engine riding mowers or lawn tractors at six years and compact tractors at nine years. Hours of use are a much better indicator of machine life than years. Hunt suggests a working life for 2WD agricultural tractors as 12,000 hours, and 16,000 hours for 4WD. By contrast, the consumer product or residential market ride-on tractors may be designed for a life

of just 2,000 hours. That sounds low, but it's not unreasonable for an owner with two acres of lawn that takes four hours a week to mow during the mowing season, plus odd jobs, to accumulate, say, 200 hours in a year. That ride-on could take all of 10 years to reach 2,000 hours!

For commercial tractor owners, other criteria govern how long they will keep the machine. These include escalating R&M costs, obsolescence due to better technology, or lower productivity compared with an up-to-date model. Others may own a tractor for just over the warranty period, then roll it over for a new one so they incur zero R&M costs and have no concerns about breakdowns. However, they do pay for it in steep depreciation.

When you are contemplating buying a compact tractor, there are five rational steps you should take:

Step 1: Keep in mind the requirements for the tractor.

Step 2: Determine which attachments are needed for the job.

Step 3: Match the correct power unit to those attachments.

Step 4: Budget ownership and operating costs for the tractor.

Step 5: Choose economically—renting or contracting may be cheaper.

Step 1: Keep in Mind the Requirements for the Tractor
Tractor mowing will be used for an example. If an area has to be cut, there is a simple way to figure the capacity and how big the equipment needs to be to accomplish the task.

Operating Width of the Mower (feet) = 10 x Acres per Hour ÷ Speed (miles per hour)

If you would like to mow the 10 acres down the back of your hobby farm in less than 6 hours, that's 1.7 acres an hour. At an average speed of 3 miles per hour, the operating width works out at 5 1/2 feet.

The actual rate of work has been reduced from the theoretical in the above formula by the field efficiency factor. For example, a fairway mowing job has a field efficiency factor of 0.7 (or 70 percent efficiency) because of the amount of maneuvering time, equipment overlap on each pass, operator, and other delays. The 70 percent factor

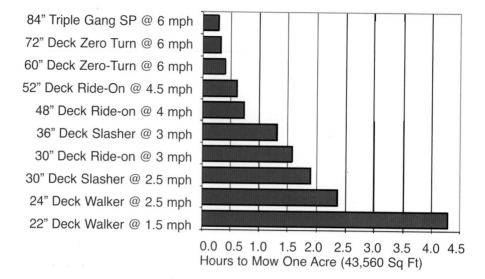

You can mow an acre with different mowers, from a small hand-push type to a 7-foot-cut, self-propelled, three-gang machine.

84" Triple Gang SP @ 6 mph
72" Deck Zero Turn @ 6 mph
60" Deck Zero-Turn @ 6 mph
52" Deck Ride-On @ 4.5 mph
48" Deck Ride-on @ 4 mph
36" Deck Slasher @ 3 mph
30" Deck Ride-on @ 3 mph
30" Deck Slasher @ 2.5 mph
24" Deck Walker @ 2.5 mph
22" Deck Walker @ 1.5 mph

Hours to Mow One Acre (43,560 Sq Ft)

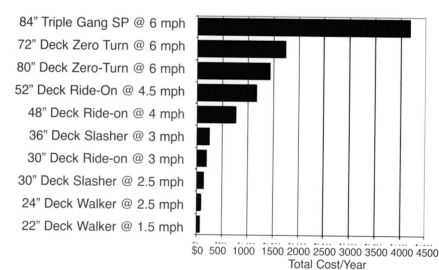

This 84-inch mower is unlikely to be restricted to an acre but it serves to show the extreme in the range.

84" Triple Gang SP @ 6 mph
72" Deck Zero Turn @ 6 mph
80" Deck Zero-Turn @ 6 mph
52" Deck Ride-On @ 4.5 mph
48" Deck Ride-on @ 4 mph
36" Deck Slasher @ 3 mph
30" Deck Ride-on @ 3 mph
30" Deck Slasher @ 2.5 mph
24" Deck Walker @ 2.5 mph
22" Deck Walker @ 1.5 mph

Total Cost/Year

is applied in each of the mowing examples in the above charts where time to mow an acre and owning and operating costs are compared.

Step 2: Determine Which Attachments Are Needed for the Job

The categories of equipment are wide and the range within categories is extensive—and you'll need to determine if tractor you consider can handle the attachments you'll need. Seek help and use common sense in your decision making. There are websites with information and useful leads. There are also resources at dealer stores, public extension agencies, and rental yards. Machine attachments may be trailed and PTO driven; or semimounted or fully mounted on the tractor 3PL (see Chapter 7). Mowers may be self-propelled or fully mounted on the machine chassis (as in some zero-turn mowers); or rear-, mid-, or front-mounted. The mower's deck size is determined by the type of mowing job and the area to be mowed.

Step 3: Match the Correct Power Unit to Those Attachments

Data on the power requirements for attachments are usually available from manufacturer's literature and specification sheets. The cylinder-type or reel mower needs the least power, and rough-cut mowers or slashers need the most power per unit of width. Riding rotary mowers, for example, require up to 3.5 to 6 horsepower per foot of cut (see Chapter 5).

SELF-CALCULATOR FOR ESTIMATING OWNING AND OPERATING COSTS
(WITH EXAMPLE)

Use the right-hand column to do your own figuring:

Sample Calculating Ownership and Operating Costs

Self-propelled zero-turn mower, 6-foot cutting width

Part A: Ownership (Fixed/Overhead) Costs Insert Your Own Numbers

These costs exist whether the machine does any work or not. Ownership includes interest charges on the average invested capital, depreciation, local taxes, insurance, and machine-storage-related costs.

Purchase Price (PP)		$11,000
Anticipated hours of use, 100 hours per year (h/y)	500 hours in five years	
Trade-in or Resale Value (RV) after five years	$3,630 (33 percent of PP)	
Calculated Average Value (AV)	($11,000 + $3,630) ÷ 2 = $7,315	
Annual interest costs at 7 percent	$7,315 at 7 percent	$512
Interest cost per hour	$512/100	$5.12/h
Annual depreciation (PP-RV) ÷ Number of years	$7,370/5	$1,474/y
Hourly depreciation	$1,474/100 h/y	$14.74/h
Insurance at $10 per $1,000AV	$7,315/100	$73.15/y
Insurance cost/hour	$73.15/100	$0.73/h
Housing or shedding cost at 1 percent PP	$11,000/100	$110/y
Shedding cost/hour	$110/100	$1.10/h
Registration and workshop costs (also at 1 percent PP)		
Add any local tax rates here if applicable	$110/y	$1.10/h
Business overheads—if conducting business as a contractor, $700 notional		$7/h
Total ownership/fixed or overhead costs		$29.79/h

Part B: Operating or Variable Costs

These vary according to machine usage and include operator wages, fuel, lubricants and expendables:

Fuel cost 1.5 gallons an hour at $1.70/gal	1.5 x $1.70	$2.55/h
Engine oil cost 2 gallons at $2.50/gallon every 100 hours	$0.05/h	$0.05/h
Lubricating, cooling, and transmission fluids 5 gallons at $3/gallon, changed at 400 hours.		$0.04/h
Filters $20, changed at 100 hours		$0.20/h
Tires, turf specials: one set of tires changed in 5 years at $200 total		$0.40/h
Batteries: one set in five years at $100		$0.20/h
Repairs, Maintenance, and Downtime (RM&D) over the life of the machine.		
Calculated here at notional 20 percent* of PP		$4.40/h
Operator's labor rate where charged		$12/h
Total Operating or Variable Costs		$19.84/h
Total Hourly Cost of Ownership and Operation		$49.63
Total Owning and Operating Costs without Labor or Contracting—All at 100 h/y		$29.53
For contracting out, add profit and contingencies. These may be calculated at 25 percent of overheads =		$7.45/h.
Therefore Contractor Charge-Out Rate per Hour** =		$57.18/h

Notes: *The RM&D costs over time are highly dependent on the way the machine is used or abused.

**The contract rate does not include ancillary business equipment or towing vehicles. If used on an acreage or earth-moving, calculate the unit costs, i.e., cost per acre or cost per ton, as well.

Field Capacity (FC, theoretical) can be calculated from FC (acres/hour) = width of cut (feet) x speed (miles per hour) x efficiency ÷ 8.25. Software is available from several sources to do the calculations for you. John Deere has a number of software programs.

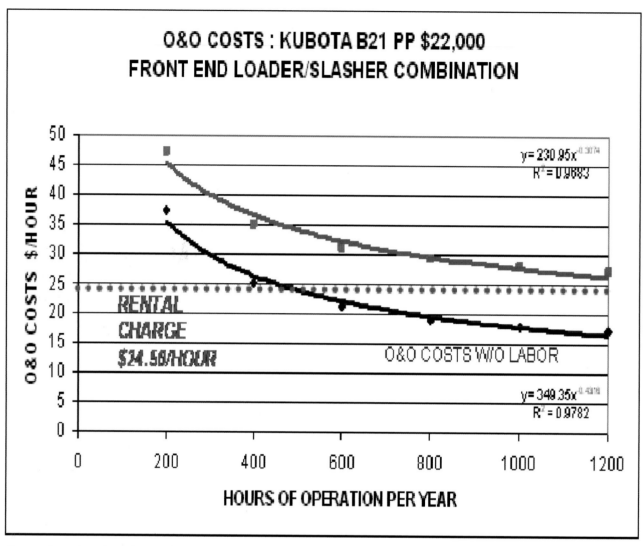

O&O COSTS : KUBOTA B21 PP $22,000
FRONT END LOADER/SLASHER COMBINATION

$y = 230.95x^{-0.3074}$
$R^2 = 0.9683$

RENTAL CHARGE $24.56/HOUR

O&O COSTS W/O LABOR

$y = 349.35x^{-0.4318}$
$R^2 = 0.9782$

O&O COSTS $/HOUR

HOURS OF OPERATION PER YEAR

These are the owning and operating costs for a Kubota FEL/Slasher combination. It costs $22,000 for a new tractor. The rental line is shown for comparison. If used for more than 440 hours a year, ownership is cheaper than renting. When labor is figured in both lines go up by that amount per hour of use.

Step 4: Budget Ownership and Operating Costs

There are three main tractor cost categories: ownership (also known as overhead or fixed), operating (also known as variable), and timeliness. The sum of these make up the total owning and operating costs for managing equipment. A bigger machine gets the job done faster, but it has higher costs. Equipment costs are often a lot higher than people realize. The ownership costs particularly hurt. Ownership costs are comprised mainly of annual depreciation plus interest lost on the capital tied up in machinery (capital recovery costs). Depreciation, which can be the highest single line item in tractor costs, is the drop in real value of the machine due to obsolescence, wear, and tear.

Since depreciation is a function of age rather than hours, it is better from a business standpoint to use the hours of working life of the tractor in the least number of years. For example, a five-year-old tractor with 3,000 hours on the meter will trade in for about the same as a tractor with only 2,000 hours of the same age, but it will have a lower overhead cost per hour. Even if you have no debts, there is an opportunity cost on the money you have invested in your tractor and machinery. Money tied up there could be invested elsewhere, so when it comes to looking carefully at all costs, be sure to charge out that interest (at its going rate) lost on the capital investment.

In a business, the main way to reduce unit costs is by amortizing the fixed charges over more hours of use. For example, if a new compact tractor with front-end loader is used for just 100 hours a year it would cost about $70/hour, whereas if a contractor used the machine for 800 hours a year, the costs could drop to around $20/hour.

TYPICAL OWNING AND OPERATING UNIT COSTS

The following gives some notion of hourly owning and operating (O&O) costs.

	Purchase Price (MSRP)	Annual Hours	Years Owned	Total O&O Unit Costs
Ride-On Garden Mower	$3,300	400	5	$9.60/hour
Stand-On ZT Mower	$6,800	700	5	$12.15/hour
Bobcat S185 Loader	$24,000	1,400	5	$16.25/hour
Deere 260 Skid Steer	$29,970	700	5	$25.10/hour
Deere 6x4 Gator	$11,900	400	4	$21.95/hour
ASV Tracked Loader	$ 26,325	200	5	$31.60/hour

Note: The cost of labor is not included.

The ownership/fixed costs accumulate day by day, even if the machine never leaves the shed. While fixed costs are practically independent of hours used per year, operating costs (fuel, oil, repairs, labor, etc.) increase in direct proportion to hours of use.

Step 5: Choose Economically—Renting or Contracting May Be Cheaper

A sample set of calculations are included in the costs table. The extra column is there for you to do your own figuring. You need to enter purchase price, hours per year, years of ownership, and salvage or residual value. Note that in the mass marketing or consumer market there are no trade-ins on riding tractors, so you may have to enter zero for the residual value of the used machine if you keep it for a number of years.

You can anticipate 20 to 50 percent of the purchase price for residential garden tractors and ride-on mowers. The repair and maintenance (R&M) levels depend entirely on operator diligence, application, abuse to which the machine is subjected, and the age of the machine. The R&M costs of heavier construction equipment can be 85 to 100 percent of the purchase price over a machine's lifetime. Repairs increase as the hours mount and can lead to catastrophic failures. By one estimate, 70 percent of equipment failures are user induced.

Whatever the situation, it's worth keeping service records. They are essential when it comes to selling the machine, decisions on replacement or new equipment investments, and at tax time. Be reminded that the mass marketers do not service products or offer trade-ins. Some equipment, such as John Deere's consumer products, are exactly the same price at any outlet.

If, after all the hidden costs of ownership have been accounted for, it's more economical to buy a tractor than rent one or hire a contractor, you will need to decide where to buy.

OWNERSHIP ADVANTAGES

Ownership has certain advantages. For example, full responsibility may cause you to take better care of the machine. There is unrestricted use, you can modify or add attachments, paint it any color, or affix your own logo.

Now that you've decided it is essential to own, there are other questions to ask yourself. Buy new or used; from a dealer or a mass merchandiser? New equipment is more reliable and comes with at least a six-month warranty. Some reputable companies offer qualified two- or three-year warranties. However, the moment the new machine is put to work, its value depreciates sharply. Used equipment doesn't depreciate at such a rapid rate. People with mechanical skills may prefer to buy secondhand and take care of repairs themselves. Obviously, the older an item is, the higher the probability of a breakdown. Owning also brings with it the need to store, repair and maintain the machine. Storing equipment under a roof pays off: by one estimate, downtime is halved by storing machinery under a roof compared with leaving it exposed to the elements.

Prices of compact tractors can vary according to where you shop. Richard Parish of LSU puts it neatly this way: "Some stores offer low prices, some a wide selection, some high quality, some excellent service, some convenient evening and weekend hours, and some offer a knowledgeable sales staff. You may find several of these characteristics at one store, but you will seldom find all at any one place." The best source is arguably a farm equipment dealer. Dealers generally offer higher-quality equipment, although some dealerships are multibranded. Farm machinery dealers usually have experienced salespersons, and they maintain excellent service and parts availability at a price. Service charges maybe in the vicinity of $60 to $85 an hour. Some agricultural equipment companies have separate lawn and garden dealerships, in addition to their farm machinery dealerships. Wherever a dealer offers second-tier

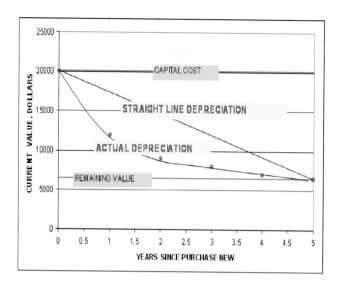

This is a typical small-tractor depreciation curve. For taxation purposes there are several ways to claim depreciation. The straight-line method is one of them; its unreal but the most simple.

brands, these are intended to compete with the mass merchandisers while the dealer still offers the sales, service, and parts advantages.

Lawn and garden equipment dealers tend to offer higher-quality tractors and excellent sales, service, and parts. They usually display quality attachments, which gives you a good chance to see what fits your job. Since these dealers cater primarily to grounds maintenance professionals and may often have government agency contracts, they may schedule service of commercial equipment ahead of yours, rather than on a first-come, first-served basis.

At the other extreme are discount stores and mass merchandisers. Their tractors may carry the store brand or a manufacturer's brand name, but their tractors tend to be second-tier, at the low-cost and lower-quality end of the scale. In most cases, parts and service are not available. The quality of advice and predelivery service are questionable. The advantages of these stores are cost, convenience, and longer store hours. Reputable manufacturers whose products are sourced from box stores will usually allow their dealers to warranty service their branded products. Check the warranty options before buying.

GRAY MARKET TRACTORS

Stay away from gray market tractors and equipment unless you have good mechanical aptitude. Gray market tractors are units that are shipped in from Asia, either new or secondhand, without any assurance of warranty or parts.

Japanese rice farmers on small acreages don't run up many hours a year and are encouraged to turn over their tractors within a few years. That means there is a big supply of secondhand machines in Japan. There are dealers who buy these machines by the container load, bring them into the United States, and after completing a small amount of work on them, sell them to the public. There are undoubtedly some very low-cost good buys, but they may not meet U.S. roadway, ROPS, or PTO standards, and some parts may never be available.

TRACTOR WARRANTIES

Reputable manufacturers offer six-months to two-year warranties that cover defects in materials or workmanship on compact tractors for residential (private homeowner) usage only. Some warranties may have an hour limitation. For commercial users, the warranty period may drop back to a shorter duration—in some cases, only a 30-day period. Reputable dealers representing those companies and who are certified to conduct warranty work offer these services: predelivery checkup; general operating instructions for your tractor; a delivery report with inspector's checklist that requires the new owner to verify and sign that the dealer has provided instructions on operation, maintenance, and, safety features of the tractor; technical support during the warranty period; and postwarranty service and parts back-up at the owner's expense.

Warranty usually covers repair of defects, replacement of the tractor, or a refund if the product does not conform to warranty expectations; but the dealer first must be given the chance to rectify the problem. In some states, including Delaware, the tractor warranty terms are backed by state law. One drawback of falling back on a warranty may involve your own costs to ship the tractor back to the dealer, as well as the lost productivity from downtime. Warranties cover compliance with state laws where applicable, such as California, to meet applicable CARB emissions standards.

Warranties are usually transferable to the new owner if the machine is sold during the warranty period. Warranties can also be extended for periods up to five years for a price. An example is $3,000 for a five-year extended warranty from date of purchase on a 25-horsepower tractor. There are some things that are not covered under a warranty. They do not cover service, maintenance, repair, or replacement by any loss or damage resulting from misuse, abuse, unauthorized repair by others, collision, or from any result other than normal usage. Wear item components are not covered either.

CHAPTER 11
ALTERNATIVES TO BUYING, ECONOMIC PERFORMANCE, AND PROTECTING YOUR INVESTMENT

TRACTOR BUSINESS PROFITABILITY

Recall the five steps before committing to a compact tractor and system purchase: Keep in mind the requirements for the tractor; determine which attachments are needed for the job; match the correct power unit to those attachments; budget ownership and operating costs for the tractor; and choose economically—renting or contracting may be cheaper.

In business, costs need to be whittled down to the bottom line; such as cost per hour of use or cost per unit of area or per ton of product. And that means estimating all costs, including both up-front and hidden. Capital depreciation is an obvious cost, but the opportunity costs of money tied up in machinery should not be overlooked in the calculations. Costs of private ownership should be benchmarked against relevant rental, leasing, or custom-contract costs. A popular size of ride-on mower with 38-inch mower deck and a New Holland compact tractor with FEL-mower combination are two examples. Note the effects that hours of use have on costs per hour. The greater the annual usage, the lower the unit costs. Labor is not included in the calculations for these graphs. If labor was included, each graph would swell by the relevant hourly labor rate.

In these graphs, the rental rate line intersects the owning and operating line at the breakeven point. If your owning and operating costs are higher than the rental or contractor's rate, you will save money by hiring or renting and not owning. But if you run up enough hours to operate cheaper than that breakeven level, then you can justify private ownership.

The shape of the graphs is completely different when the total annual owning and operating costs are compiled.

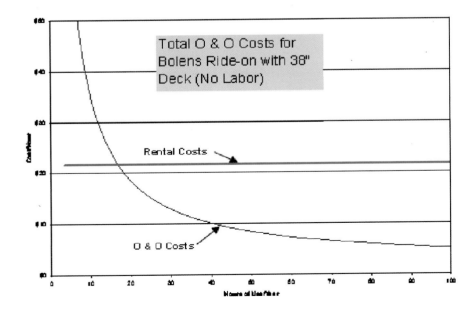

Total O & O Costs for Bolens Ride-on with 38" Deck (No Labor)

Rental Costs

O & O Costs

The owning and operating unit costs for a Bolens ride-on mower are plotted against annual hours of use. If labor is figured in both lines, go up by that amount per hour of use. Owning is cheaper than renting if it is used for more than 18 hours a year.

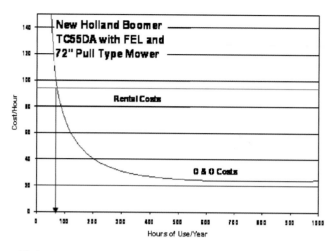

The breakeven point for the New Holland compact tractor, FEL, and 6-foot mower combination is 70 hours. If an operator plans to run more hours than that in a year, private ownership can be economically justifiable compared with typical rental costs.

The example that follows compares the costs of using one wide-area mower versus two zero-turns for golf course fairway mowing.

ALTERNATIVES TO BUYING NEW

Owning a piece of equipment implies the need to service the machine, and servicing means tools and a shop or paying someone to service the machine. With rental there is no need to have a service shop, spare parts, or special tools. Outsourcing a specialized piece of equipment can be cheaper than buying outright if the item is only used occasionally.

If renting is the path you want to take, the critical first step is to tell the rental service what you need to accomplish rather than what you want to rent. An example involved a customer who went into the store to rent an expensive electric chipping hammer. At first blink, the electric-powered unit seemed cheaper and easier to handle than the larger compressed-air hammer that he was directed to by an employee. Later he found out on the site that the air hammer did the job in a fraction of the time with far less effort. Rental staff may even volunteer answers to questions you didn't even think to ask! Reputable rental staff have considerable expertise and offer a great range or machines. They may even deliver and pick up large items such as a tractor-loader-backhoe (TLB) or a mini-excavator.

Under a rental agreement, you pay for the short-term use of equipment. You may rent by the hour, day, or longer. Usually there are discounts for monthly, quarterly, and half-yearly rates.

There are many justifications for renting. There is a diverse range of equipment to select from, including best brands. You also have access to up-to-date and well-maintained equipment that you don't have to service. There is usually immediate replacement if anything should go wrong with the rented machine. You will receive advice and training on how to use the equipment, and delivery may be part of the rental. Renting can be more efficient if you only need an item for a few hours a year.

Renting is a good way to gain familiarity with a piece of equipment to see if it fits in with your program long term. There is also less bookkeeping and good cost control, not to mention tax advantages. Personal property taxes and registration costs do not apply to rented equipment, nor does it appear as a liability on a balance sheet. With renting there is less to worry about and it allows you to concentrate on what you do best. Renting also frees your capital for more profitable uses.

CUSTOM OPERATORS OR CONTRACTORS

If you're uncomfortable with the idea of operating a piece of equipment yourself, consider a contractor. Custom operators usually bring with them a lot of experience and operating skills. Nowadays, they are taking a larger piece of the action—in some states the majority of residential lawn mowing is being done by landscape contractors. Hiring a contractor has similar advantages to renting because there is less hassle for you.

These operators are professionals. I went through the yellow pages with the notion to hire an operator with a skid-steer front-end loader and backhoe to prepare a site for a shed. The contractor instead brought a mini-excavator and said, "Wait and see!" He was right; that machine was faster, more precise, and had less site disturbance. Mini-excavators have also proven the better choice for contracting site work on sloping terrain.

Any site preparation or other preliminary work that you can do to minimize the contractor's time will be to your financial benefit since contractors are usually paid by the hour. If the contractor won't accept small jobs that will take them less than half a day, see if you can share the cost with others in the area who could keep the contractor gainfully occupied for the minimum time period.

If you are in doubt about an expensive job where a written contract is involved, ask the contractor for references and check them all. If they only give you a couple of references, be cautious. Check on insurance coverage—both yours and the contractors'—for the job. Make sure the contractor carries adequate insurance. On bigger jobs, find out their dispute resolution practices and what type of warranty is offered on workmanship. Make sure any contract that you sign is clear and understandable. If

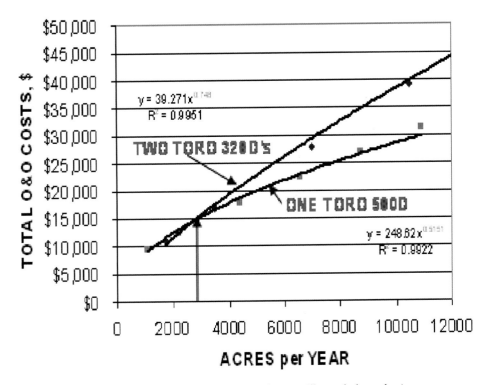

$$y = 39.271x^{0.748}$$
$$R^2 = 0.9951$$

TWO TORO 3200's

ONE TORO 5000

$$y = 248.62x^{0.5151}$$
$$R^2 = 0.9922$$

A comparison of total annual costs between one wide-area mower (WAM) versus two zero turns for fairway mowing is as follows: If more than 3,000 acres are mowed in the year, the more expensive WAM with one operator is cheaper given the inputs that were used to generate the graph.

something is not written in the contract, assume that it will not be done.

The Certified Contractors NetWork (CCN, www.contractors.net) is a nationally recognized network of contractors who focus on quality workmanship and reputable business practices. The Associated Landscape Contractors of America (ALCA) and the Professional Lawn Care Association of America (PLCAA) have recently joined forces to become the Professional Landcare Network (PLANET, www.landcarenetwork.org).

In their particular line of work, contractors have expertise, generally use modern equipment that will get the job done better than you could do it, and frequently save you money at the same time. But that is provided you can get the contractor onto your job at the time you need it done!

EQUIPMENT LEASING

In business, leasing is a way to obtain the latest premium machinery at low up-front cost. There is no down payment with a lease. Even though your monthly payments are less with a lease than payments for most conventional loans, you'll have no equity at the end of the lease. If you need equipment for a short time, leasing frees you from expensive ownership costs. Leasing benefits machinery companies by moving more equipment out the factory door. Before you lease, pore over the terms with your accountant or financial adviser. Leasing has certain tax perks for professional tractor users. You may write off the full amount of the lease in the year that you pay it. With a purchase you may just

deduct the interest payment, although depreciation is also deductible as a business expense over seven years under a purchase. When you add interest and depreciation, the tax advantages of an outright purchase might be more than that with a lease payment in the early years. However, when you lease, the lessor (the machinery or finance company) obtains the faster tax write-off associated with ownership. It may then pass on part of those gains in the form of lower lease payments. Finally, if you have no mechanical aptitude, leasing may be for you. It can enable you to run new equipment with minimal potential for breakdowns and costly repairs.

William Edwards, an Iowa State University agricultural economist, has recently analyzed machinery leasehold versus the options. He concludes that when everything is considered, the net present outlays of the purchase and lease options are close. The rollover plan is more expensive, but with that scheme you get a new machine every year under warranty. There are only a few makers whose dealers offer a rollover plan.

BUYING SECONDHAND TRACTORS

Outright purchase or getting a purchase loan to buy has certain advantages. For example, full responsibility for the machine comes with ownership and you will likely take better care of the machine. Take these factors into account when governing a tractor's resale value before you buy: brand and model, dealer relationship, and fair market value. Tractor hotline guides (see References) are a

BOBCAT SOLUTION LEASE

The Bobcat solution lease for Bobcat loaders, mini-excavators, and many popular Bobcat attachments offers cash flow, tax, and accounting benefits. Two options are available:

Fair Market Value Lease

This lease features very low monthly payments. The 18- to 30-month lease offers either 600 or 800 total hours of machine use per year. When the lease expires, you can buy the machine at its fair market value or return it to your dealer.

Purchase Option Lease

The Purchase Option Lease allows you to lease your Bobcat loader and many Bobcat attachments for 24 to 42 months. You know in advance the fixed purchase price if you decide to buy the equipment when the lease expires. Note that annual usage is limited to 800 hours.

Rental Purchase Contract

This program lets you enjoy the benefits of a Bobcat loader or excavator without making the financial commitment to buy. If, after using the machine, you want to buy it, you can apply your rental payments to the purchase price. Usually you start by paying your dealer's normal rental rate. Once you decide to buy it, the remaining payments stay the same or drop. Another nice thing is that you complete the necessary financial paper work at the start of the contract.

Four Plus Program

You can build equity in your Bobcat loader or excavator quickly with this program without making a down payment. You use cash generated by your Bobcat equipment to make slightly higher payments the first four months. After that, the payment amount usually decreases.

---

great source of information and secondhand values. Used equipment doesn't depreciate as fast as brand-new equipment. People with mechanical skills may prefer to buy used and take care of repairs themselves. Obviously the older an item is, the higher the probability of a breakdown and downtime.

There are excellent buys in secondhand equipment, which doesn't depreciate as fast, but there are drawbacks. The main one being the lack of a manufacturer's warranty. There is a tradeoff between reduced fixed costs versus the probability of higher running costs and breakdowns. It's worthwhile to pay a mechanic to inspect a secondhand tractor before you buy. Here's a seven-point checklist if you don't have access to a trained mechanic to inspect a secondhand tractor for you:

1. Overall Appearance

Check to see if the tractor is American sourced, an import, or a gray market machine. Check manufacturer's plates and serial number identification. If the plate is missing, walk away immediately! Check the hours on the hour meter and compare the hours versus the age of tractor. Does it have its original paint job or was it resprayed? Is the tinwork in fair shape? Check to see if the service record is available. This is extremely valuable. Are spare parts still available for this model of tractor?

2. The Diesel Engine

Make sure the handbrake is engaged and start it up. Let the tractor idle until the oil gets hot. Once the tractor is at operating temperature, look at the oil pressure gauge. It should be steady at the manufacturer's specification or within the green range. Listen to the engine. What is it telling you? Does the engine run evenly at high idle—no audible rumblings, knocking, or serious rattling noises? If it runs uneven or ragged, it could be faulty injectors or valves with one or more cylinders misfiring. Look at the exhaust. A diesel belching black smoke could indicate a fuel pump or injector problem. If it has continuous white smoke, switch off the engine and carefully remove the radiator cap after it is cool. Restart and look into the radiator fluid for any bubbling, which could be a head gasket leak or cracked head. With the engine idling, check the crankcase oil breather for caked oil, a flow of black smoke, oil, or water emission. Stop the engine and check the paint around the head gasket area. Is it original? If it was disturbed, be wary of the tachometer reading and crosscheck the service record. Carefully examine the sump bolts. If they have been tampered with, it could indicate a crankshaft has been replaced or reground. Refer to the service record for confirmation. When the engine has cooled down, pull the dipstick to check for black, thickened, dirty lubricant or water in the oil. These are indicators of poor maintenance or serious problems. If the person holding the tractor agrees, have a professional oil analysis. The sample should only be taken if the oil has been used in the engine for at least 25 hours. A 2-ounce sample can alert you to excessive wear in rings, valves, bearings, or cylinder walls.

3. The Radiator

Check the radiator for leaks/weeps, damaged tubes, or fins. Check the engine cooling system for scale, rust, and contamination. Check the engine cooling fluid. If oil is present, the cylinder liners, head gasket, or cylinder head may need work.

Bobcat

4. Transmission, Gears, Clutches, Final Drives

It should be possible to turn the PTO shaft with the engine stopped. Drain a small sample of hydraulic and transmission oil into a clear glass. Hold it up to a light and look for metal or other contamination. Check the transmission noise in every gear and see that each gear engages smoothly. Check all oil seals for leaks. Rock the tractor back and forth and listen for odd noises and clunks. Check hydraulics with an oil-pressure gauge and flow meter. See if the 3PL stays up or droops when the engine is stopped.

5. Tires

Check the tires for breaks, cuts, wrinkles, and buckles in the sidewalls. Use a tread gauge to determine lug depth to estimate replacement needs, as well as estimate tractor use. Well-worn lugs on a relatively new tractor indicate heavy field use. Lugs that are worn unevenly and have sharply defined edges indicate heavy road driving.

6. How many Hours is Too Many?

Around 1,000 meter hours of use with regular maintenance is low by commercial tractor standards. On the other hand, 1,000 hours without regular oil and filter changes can practically wreck a good product. Make sure

replacement parts are available from the nearest dealer or tractor mail-order firm.

7. Test Drive

Ask permission to take the tractor for a short spin.

ECONOMIC PERFORMANCE PRODUCTIVITY AND PROFITABILITY

Managers who use tractors and equipment commercially need to balance productivity against costs for optimum economic performance. The optimum is to achieve a desired work performance (tons per hour; acres per hour; contracts completed in a day or a week) at the lowest reasonable cost. The optimal performance is Machine Economic Performance = Lowest Possible Hourly Costs ÷ Highest Possible Productivity.

In Chapter 8, four ways to assess a tractor's productive performance were outlined. Each of those affects economic performance. Field performance was figured out by the simple rule: acres an hour = implement width (feet) x speed (miles per hour) ÷ 10.

Taking that one step further, economic performance for a field operation in dollars per hour = acres an hour x dollars per acre (or any other area unit). The total job cost = hours on the job x dollars an hour. Most contractors will also charge their time to travel to the site as part of the hours on the job.

For example, suppose a contractor charges $20 an acre for mowing. The total cost of the job can be figured out using the above relationship. A 10-foot slasher operated at an average of 5 miles per hour will cover 5 acres an hour at 82.5 percent field efficiency. If he spends a total of five hours away from base, the job will cost $500. Note that the contractor can legitimately charge for his travel time to and from your site.

With a ride-on mower comparison, the initial cost of a machine is simply not a guide to a productive outcome or business profitability. For example, compare a zero-turn tractor-mower that costs $10,000 versus a tractor/riding mower for $8,000; both with 52-inch mower decks and operated at an average of 4.5 miles per hour. On the face of it, both can readily cover more than 2 acres an hour on open ground. The following are actual numbers from a contractor:

The conventionally steered riding tractor/mower covers 40 acres in a five-day week. It earns $1,600 a week.

In practice, the zero-turn mower can cover 66.3 acres in a five-day week. It earns $2,652 a week using the same charge-out rate. Over an eight-month season, the earning power of the zero-turn is $34,660 more

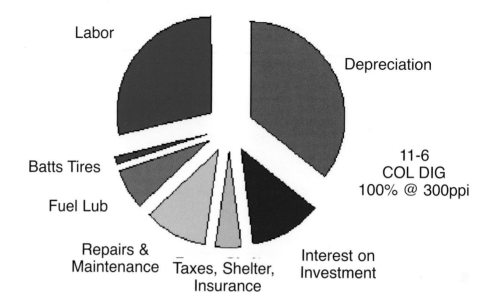

This is a typical tractor-cost scenario that shows hourly cost breakdown for a zero-turn with an $11,000 purchase price.

Labor

Depreciation

11-6
COL DIG
100% @ 300ppi

Batts Tires

Fuel Lub

Repairs & Maintenance

Taxes, Shelter, Insurance

Interest on Investment

because in reality it can work 40 percent faster in areas with obstacles.

In business it's essential to know your overheads, such as the cost of materials, subcontracting, small tools, equipment rental, and dump and disposal. Knowing those details allows an owner-operator to monitor his weekly gross profit and figure the appropriate charge-out rate.

PROTECTING YOUR INVESTMENTS

How long your compact tractor or power equipment will last depends on you! Even a top-of-line Cadillac or Ferrari needs periodic service and maintenance. Systematic maintenance will not only extend the life of your tractor, but it will also greatly enhance its resale or trade-in value, especially if you maintain a service book. Tractor service can be summarized by the acronym WOGA—Water, Oil, Gas (or diesel), Air. WOGA is a simple reminder of what needs attention at the beginning of each working day of the machine's life. It's sobering to be reminded that over a tractor's entire life span you could spend at least half as much again as you paid for the tractor on repairs and maintenance. That can be significantly reduced if you diligently follow all the manual's instructions on servicing and taking care of the machine.

Tips to extend tractor life (thanks in part to Richard Parish):

Store equipment out of the weather. Sun, wind, and snow age machines fast. A North Dakota State University study found that machinery stored indoors has a higher resale value and requires fewer repairs than equipment left to the mercy of the elements. After only five years, tractors were worth 16 percent more and harvesting equipment 20

percent more. Equipment stored indoors had about half the downtime (7.6 percent) of machinery stored outside (14.3 percent). Shelter will keep your equipment looking and running better for longer.

Check and maintain all fluids at recommended levels. Oil, water, hydraulic, transmission, and brake fluids should be checked before each use and filled up to the mark whenever necessary.

Make sure you change fluids and filters annually or according to manufacturer's recommendations. Put a service log on the shop wall to keep track of all service work. This log will be valuable if you ever trade in or sell the machine. Be sure to only dispose of used engine oil at an approved recycling facility. Oils pick up a variety of toxic contaminants such as lead, dioxins, and benzene during use, so handle with care and don't keep it around or dump it on your land.

Keep all nuts, bolts, and screws tight. Loose fasteners cause insidious damage to threaded parts, linkages, and bushings; can loosen tolerances on tight-fitting mechanisms; and will waste your time on repairs that could have been avoided.

Coat any bare metal parts—especially the insides of a tiller, shredder, or mower—with light oil. Periodically spray or put a drop of penetrating oil on every nut, bolt, and machine screw. This prevents parts from corroding, rusting, or seizing up; and it greatly facilitates repairs. Do this at least once a year or even more frequently if the equipment has to be outdoors. Apply with a pump oilcan with a flexible spout or use a spray applicator.

Grease often where zerk fittings (grease nipples) are provided. Grease not only provides needed lubrication for

moving parts, but it also prevents moisture ingress. Try not to pump in so much that the seals burst. Some equipment, such as mowing decks, tillers, FELs, and backhoes, may need to be greased before or after each use.

Remove grass and soil after each mowing or rotary hoeing. Wet organic matter stuck to metal parts promotes corrosion and rusting. Clean with a hose or pressure washer after each use.

Compact tractors can be damaged by overloading. Loader arms and tractor linkages can be damaged if pins drop out, so keep a lookout for missing lynchpins. Transmissions can be damaged by working in low gears for too long or by jerking excessive loads. It is better to tackle large jobs with finesse, rather than with brute force. Take smaller bites with smaller tractors.

Give the tractor an occasional wax or polish to enhance the paint finish and add to your machine's resale value.

INSURANCE

Tractor insurance coverage varies across companies and state lines. Farm equipment insurance is available and recommended to protect equipment investments, even if your operation is not a commercial farm. In that case, coverage may be included in your household insurance contract. Double check the contract for coverage against theft, malicious vandalism, and acts of nature (extreme weather, fire, flood, lightning, etc.). Take a good look at your deductible, too.

Comprehensive insurance coverage insures you against accidents, property damage, and third-party issues. Liability insurance is coverage against accidental damage that your machines may cause to others and their property and is absolutely essential in a commercial business today.

COLLECTING AND TRADING ANTIQUE LAWN AND GARDEN TRACTORS

Collecting antique farm tractors and garden machines has become a popular hobby. Smaller tractors are less expensive than full-size tractors and take less space, which increases its appeal. There are a number of clubs for avid collectors. Restored tractors are displayed at fairs, festivals, old-tractor rallies, parades, and charity functions. Often a restored tractor represents a good investment and can appreciate. Well-restored antique garden or farm tractors like John Deere's models D, L, and M can bring more than they cost when new.

CHAPTER 12
CONCLUSIONS

We have seen that machine ownership has certain advantages. But there are alternatives, especially if you don't have a mechanical aptitude or only need a machine for a few hours a year. Renting, leasing, or contracting are options. Equipment rental businesses are a valuable resource for compact tractors and related machinery. Home Depot alone has 800 equipment rental outlets.

There's a wide range of compact tractors and machines that use compact tractor technologies. With at least 88 manufacturers or brands, the choices are great when you consider the number of models in each brand. Faced with so many possibilities, selection is narrowed by the five P's: price, performance, power, parts, and prestige. Once a satisfactory choice of compact machine is made, you need to protect your investment and contemplate the future.

These are a few ways you can protect your investment:

Keeping your tractor under a roof is a wise investment to keep it in best-working order and preserve its resale value.

Systematic maintenance is essential for reliable performance and fuel economy.

Warranty on tractors can in some cases be extended for a price.

Your tractor investment deserves insurance protection against theft, fire, or vandalism. Tractor insurance may be possible under your household insurance policy.

Storing machinery out of the elements has been shown to improve resale value and reduce repairs and downtime. Parts such as belts, tires, and hoses deteriorate rapidly when unprotected from the elements. Places where water can collect and freeze also cause problems on outdoor items. Since a machinery shed is tax deductible for business purposes, it can practically pay for itself.

Regular and systematic maintenance and servicing means the machine will be less likely to break down and will also run more economically. A study showed that farm machines routinely maintained had 25 percent less repair costs. Timely preventative maintenance and inspection reduce problems and downtime. Problems identified early enough can be corrected with relatively minor repairs.

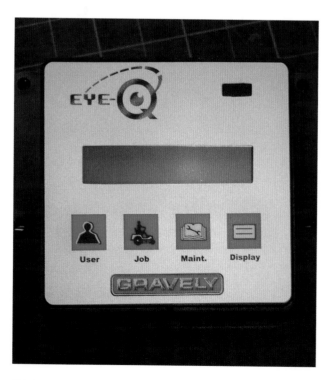
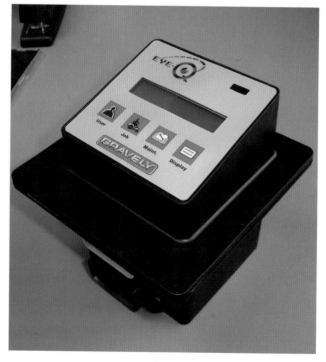

This is what the operator sees of Gravely's EYE-Q system and the potential data from the system regarding machine up time or productivity based on whether the engine is on or off. Gravely

Above and following pages: Bobcat's Toolcat, a utility work machine, has a 44-horsepower Kubota diesel engine, full hydrostatic drive, four-wheel drive, and four-wheel steer. It is an all-purpose vehicle with 65 attachments available and weighs 4,400 pounds completely loaded. Bobcat

For equipment managers, an invaluable preventative maintenance tool is routine oil analysis—engine, transmission, and hydraulics. This is especially so when more than one operator is using the machines and regular monitoring of oil change or service intervals is not one person's responsibility. Electronic service monitoring systems are increasingly available for tractors.

Engines need regular tune-ups. As engines accumulate hours, they lose power and fuel efficiency. For best service life, avoid prolonged, low-gear heavy fieldwork if possible, and for best fuel economy, gear up and throttle back!

FUTURE COMPACT TRACTORS

What does the future hold for compact tractors and machines? Unusual designs and configurations catch attention from time to time, but few oddball shapes have lasted the distance. The basic four-wheel configuration seems set for some time to come, especially 4WD with smaller front wheels. Improvements in diesel engine technologies and electronically controlled ignition systems mean that diesels will dominate the business side of the game. For the weekend warrior, the bother of dealing with two fuels will mean that gasoline-powered tractors will still be popular in the low-horsepower range and in a high proportion of the ride-on mowers. Remote engine management has been available on construction equipment and big tractors and is now spreading among compacts. Not only is the tractor operator alerted by a panel message

when there is a service need, but at the same time, the dealer can be automatically signaled.

The compact tractor market currently runs at around 160,000 units a year and is holding. Add to that number the 100,000 riding mowers, and then add skid steers and other tool-carrying machines. Compact machines are a healthy market, especially compared with the declining sales numbers of broadacre tractors. There is vigorous competition as compact tractor makers compete to attract their market share. Manufacturers are systematically improving designs, especially in the areas of ergonomics and electronics. Attachments are proliferating and opening up new areas of use for compact tractors. Changes in population demographics, urban sprawl, and the ever-growing interest in gardening and acreage lifestyles are drawing attention to the wide spectrum of compact tractors. The burgeoning landscape contractor business and the country's 17,000 golf courses further fuel demand.

Gravely's EYE-Q management system is an onboard ride-on mower computer that assesses equipment maintenance needs and analyzes mowing machine functions, productivity, and the operator's time management. The system monitors the following functions:

- OPC adjustment
- Tires
- Engine oil and filter
- Engine spark plugs
- Engine fuel filter
- Engine air filter
- Engine coolant
- Pivot point lube
- Hydraulic oil and filter
- Blade sharpening and replacement
- PTO belt
- Drive belt
- Deck leveling

A machine manager can use Gravely's time management system to determine if his employee-operators are sticking to their schedules and whether quoted times are accurate. The EYE-Q unit records when and where equipment is being operated. A GPS option can be incorporated to provide navigation, track average cutting speed, and distance traveled for each job. The hour-meter readout displays individual hour ignition, engine, and PTO times. Timekeeping functions on the monitor are continuously displayed. A shock sensor option shows if equipment is being used efficiently or is being abused. There's also a wireless remote download module called Scan-Mate that allows an individual to manage relevant information from a personal computer.

TRACTOR APPEARANCE

The appearance of modern compact tractors has markedly improved. Style has been added to function. There are racy-looking designs to appeal to the younger set and reflect off-road–vehicle design influences. The quality of finish of today's product is exceptional. There are tractors and brands, such as Ferrari or Lamborghini that are definitely designed to have high-class appeal or give the owner bragging rights in the neighborhood.

Mounting tractor attachments and tools where they are in direct line of sight has been a goal of inventors for decades. Allis-Chalmers, Hefty, Enti ToolTrac, and Landini's Pluri-Trac have their turns on the stage. Several designs are purpose built for vegetable production and plant nurseries.

MERCEDES-BENZ UNIMOG

From its outset in 1949, this four-wheel-drive, forward-control, hybrid farm tractor/truck had self-locking differentials, high ground clearance (using rigid portal axles), front and rear PTOs, loading platform, driver's cab for two people, extremely low speed for working in the fields, and 30-mile-per-hour highway capability. UNIMOG started out at 25 horsepower, but before the end of the 1960s it had moved outside our compact tractor range with higher horsepower engines. UNIMOG became the first agricultural tractor with synchronized transmission in 1959, and 50,000 rolled off the assembly line. UNIMOG is still made by Mercedes-Benz as a multipurpose, all-wheel-drive vehicle, but now it is only available in the higher-horsepower categories.

LASER MOWING

Wolfgarten Germany announced an experimental 1-meter-wide laser cutterhead in 2001 that was supposed to cut grass with millimeter accuracy and practically dissolve the clippings. It is still a prototype, and perhaps public safety concerns with lasers are holding it off the market for now. We are still left with the noisy but rugged rotary impact grass cutters. Reel mowers do the very best job of maintaining quality greens, but they are the most vulnerable if they encounter hard objects. Keeping the reel blades and bed knife sharp takes specialist shop equipment that can only be justified by a commercial enterprise that has to service lots of reel mowers.

AUTO STEER

Broadacre tractors and combine harvester owners now have a number of different auto guidance and hands-free steering

systems available to them. The day when hands-free steering will be an option on professional landscaper's tractors is not far off. One of the main advantages of satellite-guided steering is the elimination of overlap for higher working efficiencies. That would be eminently suitable for mowing and sprayer work. Apart from that, hands-free steering reduces the workload on the operator to reduce fatigue and allow concentration on other tasks on the machine. Auto guidance systems aren't cheap. They start at around $4,000 for the lower-accuracy systems on up to $60,000 for 1-inch accuracy. Radio-controlled tractors have been mentioned for use in sites where a ride-on driver is at risk.

Robotic mowers are already commercially available. So far such units are small because they are battery powered and to minimize risks to passersby from a rampant lawn mower. They are usually programmed to work in relatively small yards using a circumscribing electronic boundary loop. Husqvarna's 20-inch-cut robotic Auto Mower works without noise or fumes and automatically returns to the charge socket when battery charge is low. For absence of supervision, that's almost as slick as the sheep that were used to mow Thomas Jefferson's Monticello lawns.

What happens when oil becomes much more expensive? World oil reserves and crude oil recovery rates have passed

Heckeroth's solar-charged, battery-powered tractor. Steve Heckeroth

the point of no return in 2005. Since then, fossil-derived fuels have become more expensive and harder to recover. The first and obvious impact has been higher fuel prices at the pump. Higher fuel costs are driving manufacturers to promote products with better fuel economy, which comes from continuing improvement in engine and transmission designs. Many larger tractors are equipped with superior injection systems that produce lower emissions plus electronics that match load to speed for maximum specific fuel economy. Specific fuel consumption is measured in terms of horsepower output per gallon per hour. To save fuel, contractors, professionals, and smart compact tractor users will find ways to reduce or integrate operations to thereby reduce trips. Timely maintenance and servicing also reduces fuel costs because a well-maintained engine will run better.

Another facet of higher fuel costs is the cost of transporting food. If those costs go through the roof we will have to adapt to such change and there will be greater emphasis on local food production, and potentially, small-scale local production. Compact tractors would be a vital part of that type of economy. Alternative energies and new or improved compact tractor designs will fit well.

BATTERY- AND SOLAR-POWERED TRACTORS

There are tractors available that are battery/DC electric-motor powered, and some of the batteries may be solar charged. Advantages of battery-powered motors in tractors are that electric motors are quiet and essentially free of emissions. Smooth speed changes with simple controls are possible. The weight of the batteries are useful to improve traction, and solar charging collects free energy. Solar collectors charge best in summer, which coincides with the highest tractor use in a farming context.

Stephen Heckeroth has built several solar-powered electric tractors since 1992. The solar array actually charges

batteries, but it cannot drive the tractor alone; it's the batteries that do the driving. But time is on his side for charging batteries, and the battery weight is advantageous for traction in a tractor application. The solar electric tractor's clean, silent operation challenges traditional thinking based on fossil-derived energy because there is a virtually inexhaustible supply of solar energy. One tempering factor is that the fossil energy used to produce solar panels is very high and should be factored into the equation when great claims are being made about solar power.

Heckeroth uses a 5-kwh onboard battery pack that will power the tractor all day with light duties. A 48-inch mower can be operated for two hours and a forklift loader can work for about three hours before it needs a recharge or battery changeover. A 1-kw photovoltaic (PV) array will recharge the onboard battery pack in one day. Heckeroth claims every component in the electric tractor will operate with very little

maintenance for 15 to 20 years. An alternative 20-kwh auxiliary battery pack will power a two-row cultivator all day, a 72-inch mower for six hours, and a 48-inch rototiller for four hours. A 4-kw PV roof will charge the 20-kwh battery pack in a day. All-day operation can be achieved for any implement with two auxiliary battery packs. The weight of even two battery packs onboard is not a problem on a tractor. The PV roof array converts about 6 percent of the solar radiation striking the panel into electricity. Uni-Solar, unbreakable amorphous–silicon, triple-junction, thin-film solar panels are claimed to pay back the energy of manufacture in about two months of use. In the absence of sufficient sunlight, the batteries can be recharged from a household power point.

ELECTRIC MOWERS

Around the cities and with homes increasingly being built around golf courses, environmental issues, such as noise, pollution, and emissions, are a priority with authorities where compact tractors and mowers are concerned. Manufacturers are meeting the challenge of more environmentally friendly machines for municipal areas with electric alternatives. Using electric motors saves gas, and while the savings are valuable, other expenses are significantly higher. Over the lifetime of a ride-on mower, about 10 percent of its cost goes toward gas.

John Deere's response is the 2500E hybrid Tri-Plex greens mower. Although the machine is powered by a gas or diesel engine, it features an electric reel motor that eliminates 102 hydraulic leak points, lowers sound levels by 4 dBA, and increases fuel efficiency by 10 percent. The 2500E hybrid Tri-Plex riding greens mower is designed to meet the demanding needs of golf course superintendents and other turf grass professionals who place a high value on the reduction of hydraulic leaks, reduced sound levels, quality of cut, ease of operation, and ease of service.

FULLY ELECTRIC MOWERS

Canada's Electric Tractor Corporation offers the Electric Ox-MP towing tractor. The 790-pound Electric Ox runs quietly without gas, oil, belts, pulleys, engine, or transmission and has zero-source emissions. Its patented quick-change system—including dozer blade, mower deck, rotary sweeper, and snow thrower attachments—offers changeover times of two minutes. It can tow wheeled cargo of up to 6 tons and is able to turn within a 10-foot-wide aisle. The Electric Ox is available in two models. The 36-volt model (equivalent to an 18 to 20 horsepower gas tractor) can provide up to 12 hours of towing and 5 hours of mowing or sweeping with a top speed of 5 miles per hour. The 48-volt version (23 to 26 horsepower) increases performance to 15 hours towing and 6 hours of sweeping or mowing at 6 1/2 miles per hour. The Electric Ox uses a single pedal for acceleration and braking; it has a regenerative braking system, like in hybrid-electric cars, which captures energy that is otherwise lost during slowing or braking and minimizes the need for mechanical brakes. A parking brake sets when the vehicle is motionless, the foot is off the pedal, or should any fault occur in the control system. Optional 900 or 1,500 watt inverters enable the Electric Ox to act as a silent, standalone power source for 120-volt AC power tools, pumps, lighting, and motors at remote sites.

ALTERNATIVE FUELS

Fuels such as ethanol and biodiesel are available for vehicles and tractors. Many tractor engines have already been modified to operate on nonfossil or bioderived fuels and lubricants. Ethanol (ethyl alcohol) is one of the oldest engine fuels, but it's been held back for a time by low fossil fuel prices. It's back again with tax incentives. Suitably modified gasoline engines will run just fine on ethanol blends, although at slightly lower power output because ethanol has a slightly lower energy density than gasoline. One problem with a fuel like ethanol is that it has an enormous affinity for water, which does nasty things to engine parts. The petroleum industry has conceded gradually to incorporate 10 percent blends of ethanol (E10) in gasoline, and that caused no major problems so blends with increasingly higher EtOH, such as E85, are available at some service stations. Storing fuel on your own property has its own set of precautions, but with blended fuels you need to be even more careful of condensation and fuel contamination. The moisture that can contaminate blended fuels containing EtOH leads to microbial growth and that plays havoc with filters and fuel systems. You need to follow similar precautions with biodiesel, which is a blend of regular diesel with esterified vegetable oils. The esterification process uses alcohols to modify and thin down the vegetable oil and render it suitable for diesel use. While diesels may run on straight vegetable oil, under no circumstances should raw pressed vegetable oils be used for fueling a diesel engine if you want the engine to survive in the long term. In the Midwest, 2 to 5 percent biodiesel blends are fairly well known, and 10 percent blends are being marketed for diesel tractor work. Since March 2005, John Deere has been releasing new tractors factory filled with 2 percent biodiesel blend as part of their promotion of biorenewables. Biodiesel or blends should not be farm-stored longer than three months.

Natural gas and LPG make excellent spark-ignited engine fuels wherever they are cost effective. They have been used for years on irrigation pump engines. However, gaseous fuels do require special onboard fuel containers and filling facilities.

If alternative fuels sound good to you, check with your dealer before you change fuel types. Some engines or components may not be compatible with renewable or other fuels. There are also some changes needed in maintenance scheduling with renewable fuels. Certain lawn tractor makers offer vegetable-based lubricants for use in situations where leaks of regular lubricants would damage vulnerable turf surfaces, such as golf greens.

Fuel cell technologies are currently being revisited. There were fuel-celled tractors on test 50 years ago. With water vapor as the only emission, fuel cell power is an idea, but its technology may be held back by bulkiness, cell construction issues, and cost. Watch what happens in the motor industry, but give fuel cells another 5 to 10 years for compact tractors.

SUMMARY

The compact tractor and equipment business in all its facets is strong. A bright future seems assured, taking these developments into account:

- Growing numbers of families wanting to live on small farms outside cities
- Spreading urban blight and stresses of city living
- Aging of the population: retirees with discretionary spending power
- Growth of small decentralized food system production
- Interest in organic food enterprises
- Fuel price escalation, especially now the world has have passed the peak of oil recovery
- People spend $6 billion a year to maintain lawns
- 17,000 golf courses to be maintained in the U.S. and more underway
- Green land: the acreage of lawns, pastures, and mowed verges is approaching the size of the nation's wheat-cropping area
- Compact tractors innovations are proceeding at a brisk pace
- The expanding numbers of tractor applications and attachments

Whatever the future, compact tractors are certain to be an integral part of it.
ENJOY YOUR COMPACT TRACTOR!

APPENDIX

References, Useful Reading, and Web Sites

ASAE. *Annual Yearbook of Standards.* ASAE: St Joseph, Michigan.

Campbell, J. C. *Dibble Sticks, Donkeys and Diesels.* IRRI. 1990.

Chishti, M. *Compact Tractor Buying and Basics.* IMC Digital Universe. 2001.

Edwards, W. *Estimating Farm Machinery Costs.* PM 710. Iowa State University Extension. 2004.

Grisso, R. D. and S. R. Melvin. *Five Strategies for Extending Machinery Life.* Univ. of Nebraska Ext. Bulletin G1261. 1996.

Handreck, K. A. and N. B. Black. *Growing Media for Ornamental Plants and Turf.* NSW University Press. Kensington, Australia. 1991.

Holtkamp, R. *Small Four-Wheel Tractors for the Tropics and Sub-Tropics.* GTZ, Germany. 1990.

Hunt, D. R. *Farm Power and Machinery Management.* ISU Press. 2001.

John Deere Publishing. *Fundamentals of Compact Equipment: Engines.* 2001.

———. *Fundamentals of Compact Equipment: Grounds Care Equipment Purchasing Guide.* 2001.

———. *Fundamentals of Compact Equipment: Safety Management for Landscapers, Grounds-Care Businesses and Golf Courses.* 2001.

NRAES. "Used Farm Equipment." Northern Regional Agricultural Engineering Service: Cornell, NY. 1987.

Parish, R. L. *Implements for Compact Tractors—Selection, Use, Maintenance, and Safety.* Publication 2917, Louisiana State University Ag Center. 2005.

Quick, G. R. *Australian Tractors: Indigenous Tractors and Self-Propelled Machines in Rural Australia.* Rural Press. 1991, 2005.

———. *Compact Power Equipment for the Small Acreage Owner.* PM 1976. Iowa State University Extension. 2004.

Radcliff, R. B. *Small Engines.* American Technical Publications, Inc. 1997.

Yost, Spencer W. *Antique Tractor Bible: The Complete Guide to Buying, Using, and Restoring Old Farm Tractors.* MBI Publishing Company: St. Paul, MN. 1998.

Serial Publications

Hotline Compact Tractor Guide: A comprehensive source of specifications and pricing information on riding, garden, and compact tractors. Ft. Dodge, Iowa. Hotline Guides. 2005.

Hotline Farm Equipment Guide. Ft. Dodge, Iowa: subs@hotlineguides.com

Compact Equipment magazine and *Attachment Buyers Guide*. Benjamin Media, Inc.: www.compactequip.com

Successful Farming magazine: www.agriculture.com

Outdoor Power Equipment Institute: www.opei.org

Valuable Extension Publications

www.agctr.lsu.edu/en/communications/publications

Chat Rooms and Message Boards

Antique Tractor Internet Services (ATIS): www.atis.net

ASABE Standards: www.asabe.org

Compact Tractor Discussion Board: www.ssbtractor.com/wwwboard/compact_tractors.html

Small Tractor chatroom: www.andrew.cmu.edu/user/kb13/TF_home.htm. This site dares to provide a somewhat subjective and limited listing or assessment of which tractors are light duty and which are heavy duty; also parts/service availability. Dated 1997, however.

Small tractor FAQs; Ken Burner's articles: www.andrew.cmu.edu/

Relevant Compact Tractor and Outdoor Equipment Suppliers, Manufacturers, and Rentals

AEBI Terratrac mower: www.aebi-us.com

AGCO products include Massey Ferguson: www.agcocorp.com

Bobcat equipment, including Toolcat: www.bobcat.com

Boom-mounted Micromower: www.bomfordcenter.com

Case equipment: www.cnh.com

John Deere's full-range OPE and consumer products: www.johndeere.com

Exmark zero-turn and walk-behind mowers: www.exmark.com

Gang mowers and materials handling: www.kesmac.com

Garden tractor–trailed Tuff Vac: www.agrimetal.com

Grasshopper mower range: www.grasshoppermower.com

Husqvarna (Swedish) OPE: www.usa.husqvarna.com

Jacobsen reel mowers and Textron range: www.textronturf.com

Kanga Kid MiniLoader: www.kanga-loader.com

Kubota compact tractors and other ag products: www.kubota.com

Miniskid with attachments: www.finncorp.com

Nationwide box stores: www.homedepot.com

New Holland Boomer tractor and mower: www.newholland.com

Ride/Walk mower: www.convertiblemower.com

Shielded boom spray: www.broyhill.com

SS Cheetah Mini-Skid Loader with backhoe: www.aequip.com

Swinger articulated loader: www.linco.com

Toro's full-range greens-care equipment: www.toro.com

Trailed high-capacity leaf vac: www.trac-vac.com

Additional entries and material welcome for future editions!
grquick@hypermax.net.au

INDEX

Tools for Country Living.

OTHER GREAT BOOKS IN THIS SERIES:

How To Keep Your Tractor Running
0-7603-2274-0 • 139930AP

How To Restore Your Farm Tractor
2nd Edition
0-7603-1782-8 • 137246AP

**How To Use Implements on
Your Small-Scale Farm**
0-7603-2167-1 • 139432AP

**How To Restore Your
John Deere Two-Cylinder Tractors**
0-7603-0979-5 • 134861AP

The Farm Welding Handbook
0-7603-2251-1 • 139425AP

The Small Engine Handbook
0-7603-2049-7 • 138667AP

FOR MORE COUNTRY LIVING TITLES VISIT WWW.VOYAGEURPRESS.COM OR CALL 800-826-6600